D1526647

"Anyone who loves kids should have
this resource at their fingertips."
—*Youthworker*

"Helps those who are suffering abuse come to terms
with their situation, get help, and begin the healing process."
—*Voice of Youth Advocates*

When 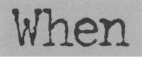 Something Feels Wrong

A Survival Guide About Abuse

For Young People

DEANNA S. PLEDGE, PH.D.

27210

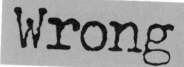
free spirit
PUBLISHING®
Works for kids®

Library of Congress Cataloging-in-Publication Data
Pledge, Deanna S., 1956–
    When something feels wrong : a survival guide about abuse for young people / Deanna S. Pledge.
       p. cm.
    Summary: Provides checklists, journaling ideas, and other positive ways of dealing with being physically, sexually, and/or emotionally abused, emphasizing the importance of talking about what has happened and getting help.
    Includes bibliographical references and index.
    ISBN 1-57542-115-1
    1. Abused teenagers—Juvenile literature. [1. Child abuse. 2. Family violence. 3. Dating violence. 4. Violence.] I. Title.

RJ507.A29 P56 2003
616.85'8223'00835—dc21   2002014060

At the time of this book's publication, all facts and figures cited are the most current available; all telephone numbers, addresses, and Web site URLs are accurate and active; all publications, organizations, Web sites, and other resources exist as described in this book; and all have been verified as of September 2003. The author and Free Spirit Publishing make no warranty or guarantee concerning the information and materials given out by organizations or content found at Web sites, and we are not responsible for any changes that occur after this book's publication. If you find an error or believe that a resource listed here is not as described, please contact Free Spirit Publishing. Parents, teachers, and other adults: We strongly urge you to monitor children's use of the Internet.

Editor's note: All the personal stories and accounts in this book are based on actual experiences. The names and details have been changed to protect the privacy of the people involved. In some cases, composites have been created.

This book is not intended to be a substitute for professional help or counseling therapy.

The people depicted on the cover of this book are models, and are used for illustrative purposes only.

Edited by Cathy Broberg and Pat Samples
Cover design by Percolator
Interior design by Marieka Heinlen
Index by Randl Ockey

10 9 8 7 6 5 4 3 2
Printed in Canada

Free Spirit Publishing Inc.
217 Fifth Avenue North, Suite 200
Minneapolis, MN 55401-1299
(612) 338-2068
help4kids@freespirit.com
www.freespirit.com

The following are registered trademarks of Free Spirit Publishing Inc.:

FREE SPIRIT®
FREE SPIRIT PUBLISHING®
THE FREE SPIRITED CLASSROOM®
SELF-HELP FOR KIDS®
SELF-HELP FOR TEENS®
WORKS FOR KIDS®
HOW RUDE!™
LEARNING TO GET ALONG™
LAUGH & LEARN™

Dedication

For Mom, Dad, and Kate—you are always in my heart

Acknowledgments

I want to thank:

Elizabeth Verdick for her enthusiastic support and shepherding of this project;

Cathy Broberg and Pat Samples for their editing skills and ability to join our efforts in midstream;

Free Spirit Publishing for sharing a vision of this book and helping to get important information out to teens;

my friends, family, and colleagues for their enduring support;

my family for teaching me about respect, feeling valued, and reaching for your dreams, all of which allowed me to complete this special project;

and to the many children, teens, and families who have allowed me into their lives through our work together. You are an inspiration.

Contents

You Can Make It Stop

This book is about all kinds of abuse. If you're being abused right now and need help, this book is for you.

Lots of people want to help, including me. But the person who can help you most is *you*. You're braver than you know, and you can put an end to what's happening. This book will help you figure out the best way for you.

If you need *immediate* help, take this book to the nearest phone. Here are the numbers you can call to get yourself safe right this minute:

1. Call the Childhelp USA's National Child Abuse Hotline at 1-800-422-4453. You'll reach a trained counselor who can help you get safe.

2. Get your local phone book or Yellow Pages and look in the front section for an Abuse Hotline. Call them.

3. Call your local police by dialing 911.

Introduction

Jimmy woke up late Saturday morning. As he looked at the clock on his bedside table, he got a sinking feeling in his stomach and thought about pretending to be sick. But he had tried that before, and it hadn't worked—actually, it didn't matter whether or not he was sick, his dad still made him clean out the horse stalls every morning and if he didn't . . . that was the part that made Jimmy more and more angry. If Jimmy chose not to clean out the stalls, or even asked to do it later, his dad sometimes dragged him out of the house, not caring if he fell down on the way to the barn, and then stuck his face in horse manure when they got there, giving Jimmy a good kick in the rear as he lay with his face in the smelly, warm manure.

Jimmy's eyes teared up as he got out of bed and pulled on his jeans; he wasn't looking forward to the usual routine, which he knew pretty well by now. After all, he was fourteen, and this had been the way life was almost as long as he could remember—at least since Mom died. She had tried to help him out, but now there was no one to turn to. Some days Jimmy felt so alone, he wondered if it was worth going on. Fighting back didn't help either. The one time Jimmy tried to stand up for himself—just last year— Dad had pinned him up against the barn wall with a pitchfork to Jimmy's chest. Jimmy was scared to death, but he didn't dare tell anyone. For one thing, the kids at school wouldn't believe him, and Jimmy was too scared to tell anyone else, but maybe he would have to do something soon, if things didn't change.

When I think of Jimmy, I feel sad and scared, not only for him but for all the teens who experience abuse like this every day. It should never happen, but it does. It doesn't matter whether your family is rich or poor, it happens. It doesn't matter whether you're a boy or a girl, it happens. It doesn't matter if you're involved in all the activities at school and make good grades or not, it happens. Abuse happens everywhere, and that is why I'm writing this book and why I'm glad you're reading it.

This book is about helping you figure out what you've been experiencing, stop the abuse if it's still going on, and start your healing process. Because abuse is such a big problem and can hurt you in so many ways, it's very important that you get help. Getting out from under abuse is too difficult for even the smartest or strongest person to handle alone. It's important to get help from a professional who knows the ropes (such as a school social worker or counselor, a county social service worker, someone in your church, or another adult you trust). However, you're the one who has to take the first step if you want the abuse to end. If you're not ready to ask for help yet or if you don't think there's anyone around who can or will help you, this book can help you get started. If you are ready for help, or already have someone helping you, this book will help you understand better how to make use of that help and what to expect as you heal from abuse.

Maybe you're wondering, why even talk about abuse—what difference can talking about it make? Some people think it's no big deal. They say things like, "You'll get over it. Lots of people grew up that way and are surviving." Other people act like talking about abuse is shameful, embarrassing, or inappropriate. But it's not! In fact, talking is one of the best things you can do to put a stop to the abuse.

I want to help give you the words to think about and talk about the abuse. Why? Because:

- I want to help you feel powerful enough to take care of yourself despite the fact that the other people in your life who are supposed to keep you safe aren't doing so.

- you deserve to feel safe and protected.

- you deserve to feel happy and to feel good about yourself.

- you have goals in life, and you deserve to be healthy and strong enough to meet those goals.

- you matter to me. Even though we've never met, I know you're a special person.

I am a psychologist who has worked with hundreds of teens who have been abused. All those young people have helped me realize just how hard it is to talk about abuse—and how important it is. I have felt honored that these teens have trusted me enough to talk about the hard things in their life. I wrote this book to reach out to young people who can't find somebody to talk to or who may not even be ready to talk yet.

Everybody has to go through life at their own speed. Nobody can hurry you along before you're ready. For example, when you learned to walk, you couldn't be made to take those first steps any faster than you did. You learned to talk at your own pace, too. Now that you're older, you're still learning things at your own speed—whether it's complicated math problems, basketball plays, or how to make friends. You can only achieve a goal when you're ready to.

This is true for coming to terms with abuse as well. You'll take those first steps when you're ready. You'll talk about it when you're ready to. One major purpose of this book is to help you move toward those first steps and first words.

Sometimes it helps to know other people have had similar experiences, thoughts, or feelings. You'll discover through the many stories of other teens in this book that *you're not alone,* even though it may feel that way sometimes.

Because of the abuse, you may be feeling angry, guilty, ashamed, grossed out, sad, depressed, hopeless, alone, scared, or all of these feelings. It's hard to feel good about yourself and your life when so many negative emotions are getting in the way. Maybe reading this book will be your first step toward feeling good about yourself. You're definitely worth being listened to and protected. I hope I can help you realize that.

About This Book

This book tells the truth about abuse. It explains what abuse is and what it isn't. It talks about the different types of abuse—physical, emotional, sexual, and neglect. People who are abused often have a lot of confusing feelings. You may even feel that you're to blame for the abuse—you're not! This book will talk about how to deal with the feelings that surround abuse. You'll also find ideas on how to tell others about the abuse when you're ready, and what to expect after you tell. There are lots of examples and personal stories about other teens who have succeeded in getting out of abusive situations and in finding help.

This book is organized so that you can flip through and find what you need to know right now, or you can read it from start to finish, like any regular book. It includes lists, exercises, and journal ideas to help you as you work through the pain of abuse, look for help, and begin to heal.

About Journaling and Affirmations

Journals and affirmations are two important "tools" suggested in this book. Using these tools can help as you work through the many different parts of abuse—dealing with your feelings, getting ready to share your story, and working on healing.

Journaling

A journal is kind of like a diary. You can use it to record what is happening in your life. The journal I recommend keeping will be a private place to record thoughts and feelings about the abuse. Some people might call this a healing journal—call it whatever feels comfortable to you. What's more important is how you use it—and that you use it. Each chapter in this book ends with journaling suggestions, under the heading "Let It Out."

If you've never kept a journal before, you may be surprised to discover how the process of writing can be a way to sort through feelings—and even to release them at times. People often don't think that keeping feelings and thoughts stuck inside themselves is a problem, but it can be. Generally, expressing your thoughts and feelings (whether to another person or by yourself) can help you feel healthier. Journaling is a way to express those feelings in a private way. It can also be a way to learn more about yourself and to begin feeling better about what has been happening to you.

Be creative when starting your journal, but be sure to do what feels right. You may not be ready to write about some of the "Let It Out" questions—that's okay. Doing what feels right is something you'll learn to practice through your own healing process.

You can write in a journal notebook or on the computer. You may be more comfortable using the computer, but many people like to produce a hand-written journal as their own creation, which can be helpful for a self-discovery approach. Find a place to journal where you feel safe. If you're worried someone at home will find out, maybe you can journal at school or at a library or a friend's house. Keep your journal in a safe place where you know no one will find it. Hide it in a drawer you can lock, for example, or ask a trusted friend to keep it for you. If you're journaling on your family's computer, store your files on a disk that you keep with you instead of putting your words directly on the hard drive. Do whatever you need to do to keep your journal safe and secure. And, if you're still worried about others learning your secrets, you can make your journal disposable by destroying the pages after you've written them. It's just another way of becoming the person you know you can be, by letting go of whatever self-doubt, shameful feelings, or negativity that may be left inside of you from the abuse.

Your journal doesn't have to be about only your experiences with abuse or about your difficult emotions. Use your journal as a place to explore what makes you happy, what's going on right now in your life, and what you dream about for your future. Do your journaling at your own pace—it doesn't always have to be about abuse.

Journaling is most effective for self-discovery when a "stream of consciousness" approach is adopted. Sometimes with this approach, strong feelings or even related memories emerge. If that happens to you, stop journaling. When you're having very disturbing feelings or memories related to the abuse, journaling is not the best approach to use. Try to find someone you trust and can talk to about these strong reactions, like your school counselor or a therapist.

Journaling as a stream of consciousness means releasing whatever you're thinking or feeling onto the written page—no censoring or editing—just let out who you are, even if it's different from the person you show to others all day long. Your journal is one place to be true to yourself, even if you're not used to doing that. You'll probably have to practice thinking of yourself first.

Affirmations

People who have been abused often have negative messages in their minds. It may be things the abuser said about you or things related to negative feelings you have about those experiences. Positive affirmations can help counter those messages and help you begin to feel better about yourself. Affirmations are statements you make about yourself that reflect you at your best and that you repeat often to bolster your self-confidence. At first, you may not believe the affirmations yourself. That's part of what the affirmations are about—helping you act as if these things are true. As you continue to repeat the positive affirmations, your mind will begin to accept them as true, and you'll probably begin to behave that way. Give the affirmations a chance to work by realizing you may not believe them completely at first, but over time you will.

You'll find affirmations scattered throughout this book, beginning with the phrase "Remind yourself." Turn to these positive statements whenever you need encouragement or a pick-me-up. Use them as reminders of your strength, courage, and value.

You may decide to copy down the affirmations that especially speak to you and your situation. Some people write them down in their journals; others write them on a message note and tape it someplace where they'll see it every day. Other people keep a list of affirmations in their pocket and look at it whenever they're feeling down. You decide what works best for you.

You can also write your own affirmations. Here are some examples:

- I feel good about myself when I ____(fill in with an activity, a place, or people that make you feel strong).

- I'm a good person, no matter what kinds of things have happened to me.

- I'm strong enough to survive what has happened to me.

***

This book will give you lots of guidance about how to start getting beyond abuse, but it's just a book. It won't make anything happen. It's up to you to take action. This book also doesn't have all the answers for you in your situation. It's important that you talk to a professional, such as a counselor, social worker, or therapist who can give you the personal help you need with your particular circumstances. Dealing with abuse isn't something to manage completely on your own. For further help, turn to the "Resources" sections at the end of each Part, where you'll find a list of phone numbers, addresses, and Web sites of organizations that help people deal with abuse.

If you want to write to me, you can reach me at:

Deanna Pledge
c/o Free Spirit Publishing
217 Fifth Avenue North, Suite 200
Minneapolis, MN 55401-1299

Email: help4kids@freespirit.com

I look forward to hearing from you, and I wish you all the best. Remember you are strong, and there are people to support you!

Deanna Pledge

Part 1

What Is Abuse?

CHAPTER 1

Identifying Abuse

In this chapter, you're going to find out about all the different kinds of abuse—physical, sexual, emotional, and neglect. Some things you're going to read may stir up a lot of emotions for you. If this happens, keep your journal nearby so you can write about your feelings, or find someone to talk to. As you'll discover, talking about what's happening is one of the best ways to heal.

What Exactly Is Abuse?

This book can help you find new ways to think and talk about what has happened to you—or what's still happening right now. Being able to recognize it as abuse and call it that are the first steps in making it stop. It can help you feel powerful to know what abuse is and what boundaries you can set to protect yourself. Even if the abuse has been going on for a long time, you can probably remember that uncomfortable feeling you first got—telling you something wasn't right about what was happening to you. It's smart to trust these feelings. They're usually right. Even if everyone around you seems to act as if it's just part of life, *abuse is never okay!*

What does abuse mean? It means that you're not being treated as you should be; this is sometimes called maltreatment or mistreatment. Child abuse is maltreatment that happens to someone under the age of eighteen. Although you may not think of yourself as a "child," or a minor, that definition can help protect you from further abuse. In the Child Abuse Prevention and Treatment Act, the federal government defines child abuse and neglect as "the physical or mental injury, sexual abuse, negligent treatment, or maltreatment of a child under the age of 18 by a person who is responsible for the child's welfare." In other words, abuse means that someone who is supposed to take care of you is mistreating you in some way, and neglect means they aren't doing the basic minimum things they should do to take care of you. Although this general description is true, each state also provides its own definition of child abuse and neglect.

Abusers may be:

- parents or stepparents
- caregivers
- neighbors
- teachers
- youth leaders
- family friends
- parent's friends
- friend's parents
- relatives
- religious leaders
- coaches
- employers
- camp counselors
- people you date

> In 2000, Child Protective Services (CPS) responded to three million reports of child abuse, involving five million children and teens. Many of those reports were "substantiated," which means authorities proved that some kind of abuse or neglect occurred.[1]

> Approximately 1,200 children and teens in the United States died as a result of abuse or neglect in 2000. Forty-four percent of those deaths were from neglect, 51 percent from physical abuse, and 5 percent from a combination of neglect and physical abuse.[2]

> Experts estimate that 12 to 25 percent of girls and 8 to 10 percent of boys are sexually abused by the age of 18.[3]

In order for the actions to be considered child abuse by law, the abuser must be an adult or at least a few years older than you. Violent or hurtful behavior committed by same-age or close-in-age peers is *not* legally considered child abuse. Yet, this behavior is still wrong. Sometimes it's also against the law, depending on the laws in your state. Abusive behavior between teens may be emotional, physical, or sexual. It often takes the form of sexual violence, bullying, or other forms of intimidation. (See Chapter 6 for more on these issues.)

Here's a closer look at each type of abuse:

Physical abuse happens "when a person responsible for a child or adolescent's welfare causes physical injury or harm to the child. Examples of abusive treatment of children include hitting with an

object, kicking, burning, scald-
ing, punching, and threatening
or attacking with weapons."
This is the description given by
the American Academy of Child
and Adolescent Psychiatry, an
association of doctors and other
psychiatric professionals. Other
examples of abuse include pinching and twisting arms or legs.

Although assault is similar to abuse, it has a different legal definition. Assault is usually committed by a stranger, or someone who is not responsible for your care and well-being, and includes some kind of physical violence or force. Behaviors in assault are abusive, and they're frequently extreme or violent. Sexual assault, for example, is often forced at gunpoint, with a knife, or threats to hit someone.

Sexual abuse means any kind
of sexual contact that occurs
between you and an adult or a
much older teen who's supposed
to be taking care of you. It can
include touching each other's
genitals, penetration or intercourse (putting something or some
body part inside you or them), incest (sexual contact between family members), exhibitionism (when someone shows you his or her
genitals), watching you do sexual things, having you watch them
or a video of sexual acts, or letting other adults abuse or exploit
you sexually.

Emotional abuse, according to the National Clearinghouse on
Child Abuse and Neglect, happens when parents or caregivers
"have caused or could cause serious behavioral, cognitive, emotional, or mental disorders" by the way they talk to and act toward
you. This means they hurt you in ways that can make it hard to
think, feel, and act normally. Emotional abuse is also called psychological abuse, verbal abuse, or mental injury. It can include
many different kinds of behaviors, ranging from severe punish-
ments like locking you in a closet to more common, everyday
behaviors like blaming you, putting you down, threatening you or
other family members or pets, or making you feel bad about yourself. Emotional abuse happens when the person who's abusing you
keeps doing it again and again and again, not just once.

> Every day, as soon as my mom gets home, she starts yelling at me—calling me stupid for not having my homework done. She never says she's sorry—like she thinks it's okay to make me feel bad.
>
> —Maggie, 13

Neglect means that someone who was supposed to take care of you didn't. The National Clearinghouse on Child Abuse and Neglect defines it as "failure to provide for basic needs, and can be physical, educational, or emotional."

Sometimes abuse doesn't seem to fit into one of these categories. And maybe you're experiencing two or more forms of abuse at the same time. That's not unusual. One-fourth of all victims were abused in more than one way.[4]

Emotional abuse can happen with almost every other kind of abuse or neglect. For example, somebody might call you names while they're hitting you, making you feel bad about yourself. Sometimes when you're experiencing more than one kind of abuse, it can be harder to speak up about what's happening because you're feeling more controlled by the abuser. That's why asking for help is so important—because sometimes you just can't make it stop all by yourself.

Could It Be Abuse?

If someone has:

- touched you in a way that feels wrong
- injured or physically hurt you
- made you feel worthless
- left you alone to care for yourself for an extended period of time

Yes, these are examples of abuse. Trust your gut instinct that something is wrong. Even if you find out that what happened isn't legally abuse, you still know that taking action now is a way to take care of yourself. If you talk with a trustworthy person, they'll help you figure out what to do.

No matter what kind of abuse or neglect you've experienced, it's always wrong. You deserve to be treated with respect, kindness, and love. You are valuable just because you're a human being. You can learn how to believe in yourself and stop the abuse.

Remind yourself:
"I deserve to be treated with respect, kindness, and love. I'm a good person."

What Does Abuse Do— No Matter What Kind It Is?

What abuse does is take basic things away from you, like feeling safe and happy—and it adds some things that make life harder, like feeling scared, angry, or nervous. Abuse hurts, and not just physically. It damages your mind and spirit, too.

Growing up in an abusive environment can make you feel tense a lot of the time. It can make you feel confused and alone. You may find yourself wondering, "How can someone who loves me be so mean to me?" These are all normal feelings in an abnormal situation. Parents, family members, and other responsible adults in your life are not supposed to be mean to you—they're supposed to take care of you.

Some of how you react to abuse depends on what exactly is happening, and some of it depends on what kind of a person you are. You may react differently depending on whether the abuse is occurring now or you're just now remembering it from an earlier time. You may also react differently at the different stages of your healing process—whether you're just getting started, or you have been working on it for a while.

Here's a look at some common reactions to abuse:

Feeling numb or forgetting the abuse. Sometimes you can get so used to being mistreated that you forget how to feel, because feeling when you're being abused usually means feeling bad. Forgetting or feeling numb helps push the bad feelings away—like it happened to someone else, not you.

Forgetting can happen with any type of abuse, but it happens most often with sexual abuse. Many people who were abused as children use "forgetting" as a way of coping, sometimes hiding these experiences so deep within themselves that they don't remember until years later, when something triggers a memory or it feels safer to think about what happened. This type of forgetting is sometimes called "dissociation" by mental health professionals. It refers to feeling separate from yourself, feeling like you're outside your body, or watching yourself from a distance.

Dissociation is a way to "escape" when something so awful is happening to you that you can't accept it as real. It means separating psychologically and emotionally from what's happening to you physically. Though the ability to shut out what's happening may have helped you get through an abusive experience, it's not a healthy way to cope long-term. A therapist or counselor can help you learn better ways to cope.

Feeling confused. It's easy to get mixed up when you're being abused, because people who abuse others—no matter what kind of abuse—usually give mixed messages. They want you to feel confused, because then you're more likely to do what they want. Sometimes they're nice and want to do things for you. They might even talk to you about what they do and apologize for it, but the next time they get angry, think you're in the way, or drink too much, they do it all over again—breaking furniture, breaking bones, breaking trust. Breaking trust can be the worst part of being abused because the effects last so long, even after the abuse stops.

It's so hard to trust other people after you've been abused. You can't always tell who's going to hurt you again because, after all, Dad, your uncle, Mom, or the soccer coach—they all looked okay; you thought they were normal. Maybe you even thought the abuse was normal because that's all you knew, but now you might be starting to find out that it isn't normal. Everybody else might have thought everything was okay, too, until somebody found out, and then the abuser might have lied, saying it never happened and that you're the liar. This may not be exactly the way things have happened to you, but these are the kinds of things that happen to most people who have been abused: *confusion, low self-esteem, a break in trust.*

I asked Dad to stop. He said, "I didn't do anything."
—RYAN, 15

Feeling scared or worthless. Abuse can make you feel scared or worthless, or it can make you feel like giving up—often the saddest and most helpless reaction to being abused. Sometimes people feel that they can't do anything about a situation, and they begin to believe being helpless is a fact. This reaction has a name. It's called "learned helplessness," and it's something that abusers deliberately try to create in their victims. Abusers try to make you believe you can't do anything about what's happening; then they can keep doing what they want. Here's something important to remember: In most cases, you can do something. You just need to figure out what feels right for you. Learning about choices and resources can help you feel powerful instead of powerless.

Remind yourself:
"I can do something to stop the abuse."

Sometimes when you're being abused, you might be afraid of being hurt again. People who have been abused often learn how to notice very small changes in the environment or in people around them as a way to survive. Noticing those small changes can provide an early warning that you need to get away in order to be safe, but sometimes the fear may become so constant that you lose the ability to tell the difference between when it's safe and when it's not. The fear may become a part of your daily life, but just because you're getting used to those feelings doesn't make it okay.

Acting out the abuse. Some people respond to abuse by acting out against others and doing the same thing that's been done to them. It's not that you're trying to be mean or hurtful, but the behavior may be a reaction to feeling controlled by the abuser.

Trying to control others can give you a temporary sense of false power that numbs the negative feelings of being abused. Feeling in control—even if it's a false sense of control—can make your own abuse seem less real. Yet neither of these behaviors (abusing or controlling others) is a useful or safe way to respond; they're attempts to act like the abuse isn't happening or to feel powerful instead of powerless. Unfortunately, it all gets kind of confusing, especially if you find yourself behaving in ways that aren't like you.

Feeling out of control. Teens who have been sexually or physically abused—both male and female—are at greater risk of feeling out of control in many ways: feeling depressed, feeling angry, feeling anxious, using sex to feel close to others, or developing eating disorders, like vomiting or using laxatives.[5] Sometimes when you feel out of control during the abuse, you try to find other things to control—like eating, drinking, or sex—but this doesn't work in the long-term.

> You can only be told that you're worthless so many times before you start to believe it yourself.
>
> —Scott, 18

What Isn't Abuse?

Teens face many challenges, including confusing relationships with parents, other adults, or friends. You may feel good and bad about yourself or others at the same time. You may feel angry with your family most of the time, even though you love them. You may feel frustrated with them for not letting you do everything you want to do. Lots of teens and their parents experience conflict. That conflict is normal as you become more independent—and your parents work at giving you more freedom. Strong feelings are likely to develop on both sides, and sometimes conflicts or interactions with your parents may seem abusive. Yet, conflict by itself isn't abusive. Sometimes teens just don't agree with their parents' rules. That's normal.

Here are some things parents do or expect of teens that aren't abusive:

- asking you to check in and let them know where you are and what you'll be doing

- expecting you to participate in family activities, like meals or shopping

- expecting your help with family chores and responsibilities

- being interested in your friends and activities

- asking about your grades

- attending school events

- helping you find constructive activities, like volunteering

What Does the Law Say?

State and federal laws are designed to protect teens from abuse. A link to state hotlines (free phone calls for assistance) is listed on page 80; you can call these numbers if you have questions about the law or want to talk with someone about abuse. Most states have laws against all the kinds of abuse we've discussed. However, some states—California, Georgia, and Washington—don't outlaw emotional abuse, and Massachusetts, Missouri, New Jersey, and Wyoming don't have laws against sexual exploitation (forcing minors into sexual activities for the profit of adults). If you live in one of these states, you can still ask for help even if the way you're being abused isn't against the law. There are other ways that adults around you can help. One group that helps with abuse and neglect is called Child Protective Services. It is also known as Division of Family Services or Department of Social Services in some states. All these groups are government agencies that work to keep kids and teenagers safe from abuse or neglect. The Child Protective Services in your community and the adults you know who think you're a great person will want to help you stop these abusive things from happening.

You can learn more about your state laws at this Web site: *www.calib.com/nccanch/pubs/sag/ define.cfm*

Healthy conflict isn't abuse, but may still feel bad or uncomfortable. Learning how to manage conflict, to identify what's uncomfortable and what's abusive, are all skills that will be helpful for you and those in your life. However, it's also important to trust your instincts. If something feels just plain wrong, trust that it is and seek help. Learning how to trust yourself, your feelings, and your perceptions is a real strength that will stay with you throughout your life.

Remind yourself:
"It's okay to disagree with my parents."

Your Rights

Children and teens have rights. In 1989, the United Nations adopted a document outlining the rights of children throughout the world. Some of the rights relating to being free from abuse are listed below.
You have the right to:

■ be treated with respect

■ say "no" when someone touches you where you don't want to be touched

■ tell someone if you feel you've been abused or neglected

■ be provided with food, shelter, and clothing by your parents or other primary caregivers

■ receive an education

■ receive adequate medical care

■ refuse sexual advances anyone makes toward you, but particularly by adults in positions of authority

■ not be called names

■ report any kind of maltreatment

■ not be abused physically, emotionally, or sexually

continued ➡

- not be neglected
- be protected from harmful situations, being abused or exploited
- develop to your best potential

Who Is Abused?

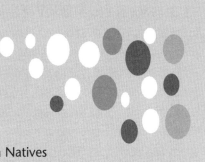

In 2000:[6]

51 percent were white

25 percent were African American

15 percent were Hispanic

2 percent were American Indian/Alaska Natives

1 percent were Asian/Pacific Islanders

***

I hope you've learned some new things in this chapter that help you feel more empowered. Knowing you're not alone, that others also have struggled with abuse, can help you feel stronger, too. You have sources of strength that you may not have been aware of—and it's this strength that will help pull you through.

Let It Out

Remember, writing in a journal is a great way to help you figure exactly what's going on in your life and how you feel about it. It's private and usually feels like a safer place to start than talking to someone face-to-face. It's okay if you don't feel ready to do any journaling. Respect yourself and your own pace. Just do those things that you feel ready to do.

Survivor is a term that's often used to describe people who have "survived abuse." One of the good things about this word is that it feels strong, and that's part of what getting through abuse is all about—being strong enough to do what you need to do to take care of yourself. Although some people like this word and feel proud about using it, not everyone who has been through abuse likes being called a "survivor." Other words people use include "victim"; yet some people don't like this word because it makes them feel powerless. Finding the right words to talk about what's happening to you—and words you feel comfortable using—is part of what this book is about.

■ Do you think of yourself as a survivor? Why or why not?

■ Make a list of ways to be strong. Include activities, hobbies, people, and places that make you feel good about yourself. You can use this list as a reminder of ways that you're already strong for yourself.

CHAPTER 2

Physical Abuse

Physical abuse includes all different kinds of hitting, pushing, dragging, squeezing, slapping, pinching, pulling your hair, or even having things thrown at you. It causes physical injury, ranging from mild to severe—it can even put you in the hospital or become deadly. Physical abuse might be something that your parents or another caregiver does to you. It's not okay for parents—or anyone else—to hit or injure you.

What Exactly Is Physical Abuse?

> My first memory of my dad hitting me was when I was three or four. He beat me. I had done something wrong—I don't know what. He hit me with his fists. Another time, I left the tie thing off the bread and he kicked me in the back while I was down on the floor.
>
> —GREG, 14

Physical abuse is an extremely angry response to normal daily life. The behavior is much stronger than it needs to be. It doesn't "match" the situation; that's part of what's confusing about being abused. Because the abuser's emotions are so intense, you may feel scared whenever you're around this person. Anytime you feel in physical danger—like you're going to get hurt—that's physical abuse, especially if you've been hurt by the person before.

Physical abuse is the hardest kind of abuse to hide. Bruises and broken bones often require medical treatment, which alerts people outside the family about the possibility of abuse. Isolation from other people helps the abuse continue, especially if it's happening in your family. The more involved you get in your school and community, the more likely you are able to find others to help you.

Nineteen percent of all cases where child abuse has been proven involve physical harm.[1]

My mom used to get really mad if I didn't get up in the mornings. She would come stand over my bed, shout in my face, and pick me up by the shoulders—I had bruises 'cause she squeezed so hard. It was pretty scary.

—Sophie, 12

Physical Abuse May Look Like . . .

- Hitting or swinging a fist at you that felt like the abuser was trying to hit you
- Shaking
- Biting
- Pushing or shoving
- Lots of hard slaps
- Pinching or poking
- Kicking
- Throwing things at you or hitting you with objects
- Threatening to hit you
- Locking you in your room
- Cigarette burns or burns of any kind
- Broken teeth
- Broken bones
- Hair-pulling
- Bruises, cuts, or scrapes
- Not letting you eat, drink, or go to the bathroom
- Making you stay outside when it's raining, too cold, or too hot
- Spanking or whipping

Who Commits Physical Abuse and Why?

Usually physical abuse happens in families or in close relationships. The law says that people who commit child abuse must be in a care-taking role, so if you're physically attacked by someone you don't know, the authorities would probably call that an assault.

Physical abuse happens when an adult or older teen in charge "loses control" in one way or another. Sometimes the abuser has been drinking or using other drugs; other times the person is just very angry. People also end up physically abusing a teen when they take discipline or punishment too far. This loss of control is not an excuse for the abuser's behavior, even though abusers will sometimes try to excuse themselves or make the abuse seem okay by saying things like "I just couldn't help myself, I lost control."

Spanking or Whippings

Spanking, which some people call "whipping" or "beating," is a controversial subject. Regardless of the words used, it means the same thing. An adult is hitting a child or teen, usually on the buttocks, with their hand or an object—like a belt or a paddle. Many adults were spanked as discipline or punishment when they were children, which makes some parents think spanking is okay and others think it's not okay—because of their own experiences. Although spanking isn't against the law in the United States, most professionals today don't support spanking as a form of discipline. It often creates more bad feelings between children and parents than good results. Spanking can create feelings of fear, shame, rage, self-hatred, and feeling betrayed by your parents. Spanking can make it hard to trust parents, and if parents overdo spanking—like when they're mad—it can turn into abuse very easily. Spanking and physical abuse are closely associated, it's estimated that as much as 85 percent of all physical abuse cases result from some kind of over-discipline.[2] Spanking is also confusing because it sends the message that violence and force—being bigger and stronger—are the ways to get what you want. This is simply not true.

Being spanked at any age can feel humiliating, especially if you're made to take down your pants to be spanked. But after about age 10 or so, this kind of spanking can also feel creepy, kind of like sexual abuse. Spanking does start to cross a line from physical abuse to possible sexual abuse at that point.

continued ➡

The good news is that spanking is on the decline in the United States. Although 59 percent of parents thought spanking was okay in 1962, only 19 percent accepted spanking in 1993.[3] (Also on the decline is corporal punishment—physical punishment—which used to be accepted in all schools. Teachers could spank students. Although many states still have legalized corporal punishment on the books as recently as 2000, it's no longer routinely practiced in most areas.)

Spanking and corporal punishment *are* against the law in Canada, Austria, Croatia, Cyprus, Denmark, Finland, Italy, Latvia, Norway, and Sweden.

What Does Physical Abuse Do?

If you're being physically abused, you probably have a lot of worries and feelings that take up a lot of your time and attention. You may be worrying about how to avoid getting hurt again. You may be worrying about whether you have any broken bones or any permanent damage. You might be worried because your body hurts. Even if you're able to make it to school, you may not be able to concentrate on the subjects, teachers, or homework. You might be distracted by pain, or worry that others will notice the bruise on your forehead, even though you tried to cover it up with your hair or makeup. You might be worried about one of your parents hurting the other while you're gone. You're worrying about things nobody should ever have to worry about—your home might even feel like a war zone because there can be so much violence.

Remind yourself:
"It's not okay for my parents—or anyone else—to hit me."

If abuse occurs frequently in your family or with other people in your life, you may have learned by now when you're likely to get hit or pushed; or you may try to keep safe just by staying out of the house. This is a really hard way to live and one that probably makes you feel confused if you have younger brothers and sisters who can't just leave whenever they want to. You may feel stuck between protecting yourself and wanting to protect them.

Physical abuse can affect the whole family, not just the person who's being abused. If you know that someone else is being physically abused in your family, you may feel sad or mad, or try to ignore it. Feelings about physical abuse can be just as hard to manage as the abuse. Worrying about whether you or someone in your family will get hurt takes a lot of energy and can make you feel tired and sad, or very mad.

> My dad still pushes me around if I don't do what he wants. He thinks I need to do everything he asks right away, and if I don't, he gets really mad and pushes me up against the wall. I've just started being out of the house when he's around, now that I can drive. Mom understands, but it makes her sad—it just makes me think he's a jerk. I don't like feeling that way, but I do.
>
> —JORDAN, 17

What Does the Law Say About Physical Abuse?

Physical abuse is against the law in every state. If you go to a clinic or hospital about an injury, the people who work there are a good source of support for you. Health care providers can help protect you by reporting the abuse, having you stay overnight in the hospital, or finding another safe place for you to be. Sometimes teens, and adults who were abused, need to lie about how an injury happened. Although teens may be lying because they're scared or want to protect their parents, being in a safe place like a hospital is a good time to ask for help. If you tell health care providers about the abuse, they are required by law to report the abuse to the legal authorities. It's part of their job to help make the abuse stop. You will no longer be alone with "the secret," and you can begin to get the help you need to be safe.

Feeling worthless and scared are other common reactions to being physically abused. If the abuse has been going on for a while, some people get angry and want to fight back. Think about your own feelings as you read through the descriptions in this chapter (also see pages 13–16 in Chapter 1). Those reactions and ways to feel better will be discussed in Part 3 of this book.

Special Concerns About Physical Abuse

In some families, teens have experienced physical abuse as long as they can remember. When this happens, some teens have lots of physical injuries. Here are some examples:

- Being hit on the side of the head or close to the ears can break eardrums, causing hearing problems.

- Shaking can cause concussions (injuries to the brain), blindness, or death.

- Severe spanking can injure muscles, nerves, or the back.

- Hitting can cause falls that may break bones, injure joints, or hurt in other ways.

If you weren't able to get medical treatment for some of these injuries at the time they occurred, they may not have healed properly. This could cause you some ongoing pain or physical difficulty. If you have some ongoing pain or other physical problems, ask a doctor to help you determine if these problems might have been caused by something that didn't heal right. Also, ask about what past injuries can be corrected; this may be an important part of your process of healing from the abuse.

Remind yourself:
"I don't have to live with pain. I can ask for help to take care of my body."

When authorities become involved with cases of physical abuse, they usually make some changes in your living arrangement so you'll be safe. If the abuse occurred in your family, the abuser will usually be asked to leave the house for a while, or you may go to a safe place (such as a foster home or the home of a close relative or friend). Child Protective Services will help make these decisions. Although you'll probably have mixed feelings about these changes, you may feel some relief that you're not worried about getting hit or about somebody else in your family getting hurt. You may still be able to see everybody in your family, but probably other people will also be there with you—again so you'll be safe. At first, it may be confusing and scary to deal with these changes. Any change requires adjustment, especially when you're not sure exactly what to expect. In time, though, you'll probably notice that you have more energy for other parts of your life, because you won't be putting so much energy into staying safe or feeling scared.

Let It Out

Remember, writing in a journal is a great way to help you figure exactly what's going on in your life and how you feel about it. It's private and usually feels like a safer place to start than talking to someone face-to-face. It's okay if you don't feel ready to do any journaling. Respect yourself and your own pace. Just do those things that you feel ready to do.

- Write about any physical abuse that has happened to you and how you feel about being treated this way.

- If the physical abuse has been reported, list some of the good things that have happened as a result.

Sexual Abuse

Sexual abuse varies greatly in severity—it includes everything from brushing up against someone's breasts or genitals to rape (a forced sexual activity, usually including vaginal or anal penetration or oral sex). Because of this broad definition, it can be hard to know with certainty that you've been abused.

What Exactly Is Sexual Abuse?

Legally, sexual abuse of someone under the age of 18 happens if:

1. The other person is at least five years older than you.

2. A sexual act of some kind happens.

- About 90,000 new cases of child sexual abuse are reported to Child Protective Services each year.[1]

- Two-thirds of all sexual abuse reported to authorities happened to people under the age of 18. Of that two-thirds, about half were between the ages of 12 and 17, and half were under age 12.

- Although sexual abuse happens to both male and female minors, 82 percent of victims under the age of 18 are female, and 18 percent are male.[2]

Remind yourself:
"I can trust my own feelings and say stop when something feels wrong."

Every year when we got ready to go to school, it was exciting, but it wasn't. I always went shopping with Uncle Luke. It was all mixed up, because I really liked the clothes and stuff—Mom and Dad couldn't buy me the nice stuff everybody else wore, like Doc Martens and cool jeans. Uncle Luke made me feel really special. But every year, the part that happened after shopping made me feel really bad. He would stop at a park close to my house—the kind with nature trails and all—and then he would lean up against me and put his hand between my legs. I was so scared I couldn't talk or even move. I almost didn't want to go shopping, but everybody else thought he was so nice, and I liked the clothes. I was afraid nobody would believe me because everyone thought he was great, but now I know they believe me. That feels good.

—LAUREN, 14

Sexual Abuse May Look Like . . .

- Tickling you too hard and in places where you don't want them to touch you, even after you ask them to stop

- Brushing up against your breasts or genitals

- Touching your breasts or genitals under your clothes or on top of your clothes

- Any form of penetration of your body or another's (for example, having another person's body parts—fingers, tongue, penis—or objects placed into your vagina, anus, or mouth)

- Forcing you to touch their breasts, genitals, anus, or buttocks, or insert body parts or objects into their vagina, anus, or mouth

- Forcing you to participate in sexual acts with them or someone else

continued ➡

- Finding ways to watch you—while you're trying on clothes at the store, changing clothes at home, repeatedly walking in on you while you're bathing, showering, or using the bathroom

- Feeling like your privacy's being invaded—you aren't allowed to close the door to your bedroom or the bathroom

- Coming into your bedroom at night, maybe when they think you're asleep, and touching you sexually

- Spanking that feels sexual

- Taking pictures without your clothes on or taking pictures that are sexually suggestive, even with your clothes on

- Showing you sexual videos or sexually explicit Web sites

- Sending you sexually suggestive email

- Talking "dirty" to you or being sexually explicit or suggestive when talking with you—like making sexual jokes around you

- Allowing or forcing you to watch them have sex or masturbate (sexual self-stimulation), or forcing you to touch yourself in front of them

Who Commits Sexual Abuse and Why?

Sexual abuse is committed by all different kinds of people. However, studies show that most abusers are male (94 percent) and are more likely to have been sexually abused themselves. Female offenders are more common with children under age 6; however 6 percent of people who abused older minors were female. Family members most often abuse younger children—42 percent for children between the ages of 6 and 11—while only 24 percent of abusers are family members for those between the ages of 12 and 17.[3]

Other studies show a connection between poor social skills and abusing others. In other words, many people who abuse have a hard time relating to others as "real" people, understanding or caring about how their actions affect others. People who commit sexual abuse usually know their victim. Most child sexual abuse occurs in somebody's home and doesn't include a weapon. Adults who abuse children and teens usually use their adult status to intimidate or scare their victim into doing what they want.

My brother used to take me down to the drainage ditch. He made me do it with him. It hurt, but he's a lot bigger than me, so I couldn't stop him. Mom and Dad always tell me I have to mind John because he's my brother. Is this what they meant? Now I wonder if I'm gay—I want to go out with girls, but that feels weird now. Sometimes I feel like I really hate my brother for doing this to me.

—BOBBY, 13

What Does Sexual Abuse Do?

Sexual abuse can make you feel like you don't have any control over your life, that no one cares about you, or that those who do care are also powerless. Sexual abuse takes away your freedom to explore who you are because you're thinking about ways not to get abused or to keep your abuser happy.

Remind yourself:
"I have a purpose in life. Nobody's going to stop me from finding out what it is and achieving it."

Sexual abuse often causes feelings of:

- fear
- anxiety
- depression
- anger
- hostility
- poor self-esteem

How you react to being sexually abused depends on a lot of different things. For example, if you were abused by someone in your family, it may be really hard to trust others. You may feel betrayed.

You may even question whether you can trust your own judgment. Individual reactions can be so different that you may feel alone because no one else seems to be reacting as you are.

If you felt threatened or scared by the abuse, you may have a hard time forgetting or you may not remember details of what happened. Forgetting about the abuse is called dissociation (see Chapter 1, pages 13–14).

Sexual abuse may make you feel bad about yourself or, when you're older, confused about having sex in a healthy relationship when it should be okay. Other people who have been sexually abused have sex more often and more carelessly, like choosing not to have safe sex. Other careless behaviors that are self-destructive—such as drinking, using other drugs, or harming oneself—are also more likely in people who have been sexually abused. (See Chapter 17 for more about unhealthy ways that people cope with abuse.)

Sexual abuse can feel very confusing as well, making you question your decisions, your ability to take care of yourself, or your ability to do things that are good for you. One thing that's especially confusing is that sometimes what the abuser does feels good. Here's something important to remember: You can't help it that your body feels good when you're touched (whether in a sexual way or not). That's just the way our bodies are wired. Still, it feels confusing if the good feelings happen as a result of bad touch. Just keep in mind that it doesn't mean the abuse is your fault just because it may feel good to your body.

Sexual abuse can also seem more confusing than other types of abuse because you may just be starting to figure out how to even be around people you're attracted to. All those new feelings are confusing enough, but when an adult is also touching you or acting in a way that feels weird or uncomfortable, you may feel completely frozen. You may have no idea what to do.

Here's an example of how sexually abusive behavior can be confusing for teens: Suppose Uncle Harry always sits right next to you—so close that you smell his aftershave—and it makes you feel completely creepy. Then he asks you to sit on his lap, like when you were five—but now you're 15. Nobody stops it. Your grandma actually thinks it's cute. Nobody's supporting you. In such a situation, it's okay to excuse yourself and walk away. Say: "I'm going to check on something with my dad," or "I need to look in the kitchen for Mom." It feels scary because nobody seems to "get it." You probably question yourself, too, but trusting your instincts is the best thing to do. If it feels creepy to be around Uncle Harry, follow your feelings and don't do what he asks. Even though other people in your family are in the same room, they may just not understand because they don't think of Uncle Harry that way, they don't have good sexual boundaries themselves, or they think his behavior is "harmless." You

What Does the Law Say About Sexual Abuse?

Although laws vary somewhat from state to state, a generally accepted definition of sexual abuse is "a sexual act directed against another person, forcibly and/or against that person's will; or against the person's will without force where the victim is incapable of giving consent because of his/her youth."[4]

may need to talk to Mom, Dad, or Grandma and tell them how you feel. If they don't understand and help you, keep more distance from the abuser, whether or not someone else is around.

Remind yourself:
"Even though I feel alone, there are people who can help me."

After a while I just got used to what happened when my cousin and his gang would come over. I tried to fight it at first, but there were too many of them. I just gave up.

—TAMEIKA, 16

Special Concerns About Sexual Abuse

> Dad touched my privates and stuff like that while I
> was in the bathtub.
>
> —Charlie, 15

Incest

Incest means sexual abuse by a family member. The most common abuser in cases of incest is a father or father figure (this includes stepfathers or Mom's live-in boyfriends). It's also called incest when sexual activity occurs between siblings or cousins of different ages.

Incest is often a closet secret in families, because family members are supposed to protect and take care of each other—not take advantage of each other. Incest is hard on so many levels.

Part of what's so confusing about incest is that it may take a while to figure out that it's not okay—that this doesn't happen in all families or that this isn't how people show they care about you. Incest often begins when children are very young, so they may grow up with this kind of behavior, not knowing anything differently until many years later. The abuser usually works hard to keep the incest a secret.

Incest:

■ breaks many different kinds of trust

■ takes advantage of you

■ stops you from being who you are and can be

> Dad made me rub his private part once, after he
> moved out. He said he loved me and asked if it felt
> good. It was so gross—I cried.
>
> —Jane, 14

These are just a few reasons incest needs to stop. The bad feelings that you have every day—trying to avoid being at home or around the person, thinking it's your fault, thinking you're worthless or bad, being afraid, the confusion you might feel if you have sexual feelings you enjoy while being abused—are too stressful. Stress and bad feelings can even make you unhealthy. You're worth more than that.

Rape

Rape means forced sex, or intercourse. This includes penetration of the vagina or anus (sodomy) with a penis or an object. Oral sex that is forced is also rape. When an adult has sexual intercourse or oral sex with a minor, or someone legally defined as a child, it's called statutory rape. Date rape, also called acquaintance rape, occurs when you feel forced, coerced, or pressured into sex with someone you know. If you said no to having sex and it happens anyway, that is date rape. (See Chapter 6 for more on date rape.)

> I don't trust anybody anymore. My ex-boyfriend came over late one night. He wanted to have sex and I didn't—I said "no"—but he wouldn't listen to me. He held me down and made me have sex. He raped me.
>
> —BONITA, 16

Of all rapes that are reported to legal authorities, 67 percent happen to people under the age of 18; 34 percent happen to kids under 12.[5] These numbers mean that most of the rapes that are reported happen to people who are still in high school.

Many people who have been raped struggle with feelings of vulnerability, not feeling safe, or feeling scared more often. You may also be asking yourself:

- Can I have children?
- Am I damaged?
- Will anyone want me?

Usually, females who have been raped can have children. Although there may be physical injury or bruising, you're not damaged. You just need time to heal. You're not unlovable because of what happened. You didn't choose for this to happen, and you're still the same special person you were before.

***

Keeping your feelings inside about sexual abuse is really hard and unhealthy. If something has happened to you that doesn't feel right, talking about it with a trustworthy person will help you feel better. Try not to let what other people think keep you from taking care of yourself—that's what real strength is about.

Let It Out

Remember, writing in a journal is a great way to help you figure exactly what's going on in your life and how you feel about it. It's private and usually feels like a safer place to start than talking to someone face-to-face. It's okay if you don't feel ready to do any journaling. Respect yourself and your own pace. Just do those things that you feel ready to do.

- How does having a label for your experiences feel?

- "Strength is in numbers." Write about how it feels to know what's happened to you has happened to others.

CHAPTER 4

Emotional Abuse

Many people get so used to being treated badly that they don't think there's anything wrong with it, but there is. Emotional abuse can really hurt, but unlike some other forms of abuse, there's no physical sign that it's happening. Emotional abuse is tough stuff that can make you feel really alone, and really bad about yourself.

What Exactly Is Emotional Abuse?

> Growing up with my stepfather was like going through the military at the age of 10. If I didn't act a certain way, he said I was annoying or out of line. He would tell my mom he was sorry for saying this stuff but later find me when I was alone and yell at me for being such a crybaby.
>
> —Pablo, 18

Emotional abuse happens when someone yells at you, calls you names, or makes you feel stupid or worthless again and again and again, not just once. Emotional abuse can be either verbal—using negative words or name-calling—or nonverbal, like giving you a certain look. It can include rejecting, ignoring, terrorizing, isolating, corrupting, or exploiting you. Emotional abuse is the most common type of abuse and often occurs at the same time as other types of abuse. For example, someone may hit you and yell at you simultaneously. Emotional abuse may even make you feel worse about yourself than other kinds of abuse.

Here's a closer look at each of those types:

Rejecting emotional abuse includes behaviors that make teens feel like their parents, other adults, or friends don't want them, are pushing them away, just don't want to be around them, or think they're not good enough. People who are rejecting may make you feel like you can't live up to their expectations. The rejection may be subtle or more direct, such as calling you names, saying you're worthless, refusing to talk to you, or acting as if you're to blame for anything that goes wrong.

> Everything I did was wrong. My dad never said anything about it—he just wouldn't talk to me. Why that made me so upset, not mad, but sad, I'll never know. I didn't want him mad at me, so I did what I could to keep him happy with me.
>
> —Sue, 17

Ignoring emotional abuse happens when important people in your life aren't nurturing or act like they're not interested in you. Actual ignoring—not acknowledging your presence or feelings—sometimes happens, too. Even though they may be physically present, it feels like they're not there for you emotionally.

> I remember when I was in third grade. It was Valentine's Day and my night to visit my dad. He got mad at me because I didn't bring my Valentines from school to show him, and he wouldn't talk to me all night long. My stepmom was just as bad. She wouldn't talk to me either, or she would yell at me behind his back. All I ever tried to do out there was not make anybody mad, because if I did, they'd make me feel like I did something wrong. Sometimes it was better when they ignored me.
>
> —Libby, 16

Terrorizing behavior can make you feel singled out for criticism or punishment. You may be ridiculed for displaying normal feelings, or it may seem like others have unrealistic expectations for you—like you can never figure out how to be successful or win their approval. The terror may feel like something is scary or threatening, as if you're going to be physically hurt. You may be threatened with death, mutilation, abandonment, or a threat to hurt others you love. This type of threat often happens with sexual abuse or physical abuse.

Isolating behavior often happens in families or relationships where other forms of abuse are going on, too. Parents who isolate may not let you go out and do things that are normal for teens. They may lock you in your room or make you eat by yourself. The isolation helps the abuser feel in control and actually makes it easier for the abuser to keep abusing you, because other people don't know what's going on.

Corrupting or exploiting behaviors happen when boundaries are blurred. That means parents have trouble acting like parents, and you may feel like you're the parent or that you don't have a parent. Other adults may treat you like an equal by letting you drink or smoke with them, or by being sexually suggestive. Although some parts of this type of abuse may sound good—because you could do anything you want—it can also be scary and dangerous. Parents or other adults aren't setting healthy boundaries when, for example, they allow teens to use drugs or alcohol, watch cruel or violent behavior, view pornographic material, or participate in criminal activities. Exploiting behaviors can include allowing or forcing teens to be used for sex or as prostitutes.

What Emotional Abuse May Look Like . . .

- Name-calling
- Saying or doing things that make you feel stupid or worthless, like saying you'll never be good at anything or you can't do anything right
- Making fun of things you're sensitive about—like your weight or grades or even how you do things around the house

continued ➡

- Making you feel like you have to do things a certain way or they'll get mad

- Making you feel like what they want is more important than what you need to do—like making you stay home from school to clean the house or take care of brothers or sisters again and again and again

- Not allowing you to spend any time outside of school with your friends or other people your age

- Making you feel scared or nervous about your choices or actions, like you aren't good enough or you are wrong

- Being ignored by your parents when you tell them how you feel, or they make you think your feelings are "stupid" or don't matter

- Parents not making you feel loved or cared about

- Refusing to talk to you when you've done something they don't like

Who Commits Emotional Abuse and Why?

People who emotionally abuse teens are often family members, even parents. Sometimes they're not aware of what they're doing— they don't realize the pain they're causing you. That doesn't make it okay. But parents who emotionally abuse their children often have problems taking care of their own emotional needs and, therefore, don't know how to treat their children in a positive and supportive way. It's important to remember that someone's lack of knowledge doesn't excuse his or her abusive behavior.

Emotionally abusive relationships can happen outside families, too. In fact, nonfamily members commit this kind of abusive behavior more often than any other kind. Emotionally abusive behavior in peer relationships or dating is similar to bullying. It occurs in schools and the workplace. When lots of other people act this way toward you, it's called "mobbing." If you've ever been ganged up on and intimidated by other students, that's mobbing— sort of like group bullying. Emotional abuse is common in dating relationships, when one person tries to control the other by making them question themselves or feel badly about themselves. (See Chapter 6 to learn more about these issues.)

Remind yourself:
"I can feel good about myself, no matter what other people tell me."

What Does Emotional Abuse Do?

Emotional abuse can negatively affect how you develop and how you feel about yourself. After repeated emotional abuse, teens often come to see themselves as unworthy of love, affection, or many good things that are a normal part of life.

> My dad wasn't around much, but when he was, all he would do was yell at me. He'd call me names and tell me how stupid I was, but then he'd ask me to read him the newspaper because he couldn't. It made me so mad, like he was using me, but I knew I couldn't say anything because he'd just tell me how worthless I was. The only time he noticed me was when he thought I did something wrong.
>
> —JASON, 15

Being around an abusive person usually makes you feel like you don't know what's going to happen next—you may feel kind of nervous most of the time. One thing you do know is how awful it feels when the person says or does these hurtful things to you. It's hard to feel good about yourself, because it feels like these important people don't care about you or respect you. It can make you feel kind of sad, angry, or unmotivated.

Emotional abuse can also make you feel anxious and insecure about yourself and your relationships with others. It can even lead to physical problems, such as stomachaches or headaches. Some people say that emotional abuse leaves "hidden scars":

- insecurity
- low self-esteem

- destructive behavior
- angry acting out (such as fire-setting or cruelty to animals)
- withdrawal
- developmental delays
- substance abuse
- suicidal thoughts
- symptoms of depression
- anxiety
- difficulty forming relationships

What Does the Law Say?

It's difficult to take legal action for emotional abuse because this form of abuse is hard to prove (from a legal perspective). That doesn't mean you can't get help. Child Protective Services can still become involved and help set up treatment or provide a safer place for you to live for a period of time. Don't give up hope just because the legal system isn't able to do as much—there are other agencies and people who can help.

When people abuse you in this way, you may become overly sensitive to the cues of others and less aware of your own likes and dislikes. You do this in order to avoid their angry response—even if it's silence.

Remind yourself:
"I can get support from people outside my family."

Special Concerns About Emotional Abuse

One of the hard things about emotional abuse is that you may begin to believe all the bad things that others say or imply about you. You may begin to believe that you're not smart or talented enough to reach your goals or that you're not capable of making changes in your life. Those feelings take away some of your personal power. Emotional abuse is far more serious and damaging than the old saying "Sticks and stones may break my bones but words will never hurt me." Scientists are discovering the power of words and thoughts to hurt us or help us. Studies show the effectiveness of positive thoughts, feelings, and words—even when someone faces cancer or major surgery. The opposite is also true, and that's part of the challenge of healing and moving forward from abuse.

What's important is how you feel about yourself, not what others tell you about yourself. Even though you may not believe good things about yourself right now, with practice, you will. You can begin countering the negative messages you're hearing by identifying your strengths.

Remind yourself:
"How I feel about myself is what's important."

Let It Out

Remember, writing in a journal is a great way to help you figure exactly what's going on in your life and how you feel about it. It's private and usually feels like a safer place to start than talking to someone face-to-face. It's okay if you don't feel ready to do any journaling. Respect yourself and your own pace. Just do those things that you feel ready to do.

■ After recognizing that you've been emotionally abused, it's important to separate what's being said about you from how you feel about yourself, or how you want to feel about yourself. Make a list for each category ("What's Been Said," "How I Feel About Myself," and "How I Want to Feel About Myself") to help visualize the difference.

■ What things do you do for yourself that help you feel special and strong?

CHAPTER 5

Neglect

Neglect means that your parents or guardians aren't taking care of you the way they're supposed to. It's not that you aren't getting what you want—you aren't getting what you need.

What Exactly Is Neglect?

Parents are to provide all kinds of things for their kids:

■ a safe place to live

■ food and clothes

■ health care

■ an opportunity to attend school

■ help if you have addictions or need other treatment

■ love and affection

When parents don't do those things for you on a regular basis, they may be neglecting you. Neglect is considered a pattern—in other words, any of these things not being taken care of has to occur repeatedly over a period of time. Neglect isn't just something that happens once or twice. If you're in a situation where you're being neglected, it's probably been happening for most of your life.

> Sometimes it feels like my parents don't care about me. Dad's at work all the time, or he and Mom go to charity events around town. I'm always fixing dinner for my little brother and me—like three or four times a week. It never used to happen like this, but it's been this way all school year, and that's been almost 9 months now.
>
> —BECKY, 13

Here are four types of neglect:

Emotional neglect is when your parents or caretakers don't pay a lot of attention to you. They may not get you counseling if you need it, they abuse other people

> Neglect is the most common form of abuse today. In 2002, neglect accounted for nearly two-thirds of substantiated cases of child abuse.[1]

in front of you, or they let you use drugs and alcohol. Emotional neglect is different from emotional abuse. Someone who emotionally abuses you makes you feel bad, like name-calling, but emotional neglect is leaving you alone too much. Even babies need to have other people talk to them, touch them, and help them feel important and capable. We never stop needing those things.

Educational neglect means your parents or guardians aren't making sure you're attending school, they're having you stay at home instead of going to school, or they're not taking care of getting you the special services you need at school.

Physical neglect includes any act of not caring for your physical needs, such as housing, clothing, or food. It includes leaving you to take care of yourself or your younger brothers and sisters on a regular basis (not just after school), kicking you out of the house or not letting you come back after you've run away, or letting you do whatever you want whenever you want (you may like the sound of this last one, but it's a form of neglect, too).

> I quit school last year because my mom started using drugs—then she was never around. I couldn't let my little brother stay there by himself—he's only in fourth grade. There was nobody around to fix him dinner or buy food, or make sure he got to school, so I got a job to support the two of us. Mom still shows up sometimes, but she's just gone most of the time. I wanted her to get some help, but she never stays around long enough.
>
> —RAMONE, 17

Medical neglect includes not taking care of medical needs, such as not getting necessary immunizations or not going to the doctor or dentist soon enough after an injury. (Some families follow religious guidelines that don't allow certain types of medical interventions, so there can be some exceptions. However, there is controversy and disagreement about these exceptions.)

> Some of the kids make fun of me at school because of my teeth. One fell out last week. My mama never takes me to the dentist, so my teeth get bad and they hurt. I can't sleep when I get a toothache, and I don't like to go to school much then either. I just stay at home sometimes. Mama doesn't care.
>
> —Shameika, 14

Remind yourself:
"It's normal to still need my parents.
I don't need to do everything myself."

Neglect May Look Like . . .

- Not providing for your basic survival needs—like food, shelter, or clothing

- Not making arrangements for a safe, clean place to live

- Not providing for things you need—like clothes or school supplies (an exception is when your family has an agreement that you pay for some things yourself, with a part-time job, for example)

- Not making sure you're as safe as can be planned for

- Not providing adequate supervision, or leaving you alone for long periods of time, like overnight every night or most nights

continued ➡

- Not taking you to the doctor or dentist when you need medical care—like after a broken bone or when you have a bad cough
- Not taking care of eye exams or glasses, if you need them
- Making you wear clothes that are way too small, too big, or are dirty
- Not having enough food in the house for you to eat

Who Neglects and Why?

Any adult who is supposed to take care of you, but doesn't, is neglecting you. It could be your mom, dad, or a guardian or caretaker such as an aunt or uncle.

As with emotional abuse, many parents or other caretakers may not know that they're being neglectful. This can happen for many reasons. Sometimes neglect happens because parents can't afford to take care of you in the way they should, and sometimes, it's because they may be too busy doing other things besides being a parent. Other times, parents may be "impaired," making it difficult for them to do a good job of being parents. Parents who are impaired may have problems with substance abuse, like drinking or being addicted to drugs. They may struggle with a mental illness, such as severe depression or schizophrenia. Parents may have medical conditions that make it hard for them to be a parent—like chronic pain or heart problems. Some parents just don't have very good parenting skills, and don't know how to take care of their children.

None of these reasons justify neglect. Just like abuse, neglect is never okay.

What Does Neglect Do?

When you're neglected, sometimes you have to act kind of like another parent—because somebody needs to fill that role. You may be taking care of the house, talking to bill collectors, doing the grocery shopping and cooking, or caring for your brothers and sisters. Although most teens do some of these things some of the time to help out, none of those jobs is yours to do on a regular basis. Basic physical, emotional, or intellectual needs aren't being met in a family where there is neglect.

Parents who are dealing with money problems might try to avoid the bad feelings by drinking, using other drugs, or being gone a lot. Some parents might even try to support the family or their drug habits with prostitution. Any of these situations may make you feel unsafe and neglected.

How people respond to neglect depends on their assumptions about why it has happened and how long it's been going on. Neglect can make some teens more determined to get out of a negative life situation, or just to take positive control over their lives. Getting help to make these positive changes is a good idea. Child Protective Services can be a good resource, so you don't have to do it alone.

If neglect is extreme, has gone on for a long time, involved lack of food, inadequate medical attention, unsafe living conditions, or not going to school, there may be permanent, long-term effects. When bodies don't get enough nourishment during the early stages in life, they don't grow as well as they should. This can affect your body's appearance, how your internal organs function, and how your brain works. Also, being hungry can distract you from the things you should be focusing on—like your schoolwork. Unsafe living conditions can make you feel nervous much of the time. Missing a lot of school or dropping out can make it hard to get a job or reach your dreams later in life. If neglect is not as extreme, the effects may be temporary and you can "catch up" in these areas. Neglect just makes life harder because you don't have all the tools or support you need to be your best.

Like other forms of neglect, medical neglect makes it hard for you to do your best, because your basic physical needs for a healthy body aren't being met. It's kind of like being half-asleep at school or not having a book, paper, or pencil to do your work. If your body isn't functioning well, it's a lot harder to succeed because you don't have everything you need.

What Does the Law Say?

Parents have a legal obligation to care for their children and meet their basic needs until the children are legally considered adults, usually at 18. Neglect is the most common form of maltreatment reported to authorities; however, prosecution rarely happens. Usually a surprise visit to the

continued ➡

home is the first part of an investigation by Child Protective Services. Investigators have to determine if neglect is actually happening. They have to decide whether the living conditions are the result of poverty or lifestyle, or a combination of factors. Unsafe conditions include exposed electrical wires, rats or roaches in the home, or really unclean conditions.

Child Protective Services or other authorities will not remove children or teens from a home unless they think they are in immediate danger. You may remember from Chapter 1 Child Protective Services is a government agency designed to protect the well-being of children and adolescents. In some states Child Protective Services is part of other agencies, such as the Division of Family Services or the Division of Youth Services. Once you choose to talk about your abuse with a responsible adult, a professional from Child Protective Services who works with abuse cases will usually be the next person who will talk with you about your abuse. Keeping families together is the primary goal for family service agencies such as these, and most will try to help the family improve the situation in the home. Authorities may temporarily place children elsewhere if

- the children are very young

- the adults are using drugs or drinking to the extent that it impairs their ability to parent

- the adults have been arrested and no other family members are available for supervision

Special Concerns About Neglect

Teens who are being neglected at home often end up taking too much responsibility there, because their parents aren't. Switching family roles—teens acting like parents and parents acting like children—upsets normal family relationships. If you're taking on too much responsibility for your age—acting like an adult—then you aren't able to focus on what you need to be doing for yourself. You need to learn things at school, play sports, get involved in school clubs, and have fun with other people your age. You'll have time to be an adult later. It's your parents' turn to be adults right now. Feeling so much pressure can make it hard for you to do what you need to do for yourself and may make you feel sad, mad, or nervous. Those are normal feelings when you're being pushed to do more than is appropriate for your age.

Remind yourself:
"It's my turn to be a teenager."

You may feel down or hopeless as a result of neglect. Some of these feelings can result from knowing that you don't have the same chances as other people your age or that you're doing more than everybody else you know. Sad, angry, or hopeless feelings can be part of neglect. The combination of strong feelings, extreme pressures, and the stress of doing a lot can sometimes lead to more family conflict. When you ask for help, you can learn ways to feel better about yourself, and the other people in your family can learn how to be more supportive of each other, too.

Remind yourself:
"I can ask for what I need, and people will help me."

Let It Out

Remember, writing in a journal is a great way to help you figure exactly what's going on in your life and how you feel about it. It's private and usually feels like a safer place to start than talking to someone face-to-face. It's okay if you don't feel ready to do any journaling. Respect yourself and your own pace. Just do those things that you feel ready to do.

■ It's not fair that some of your needs haven't been met. It can be especially hard when you see people on television or in your school who seem to have everything they need and want. Write about your feelings about being neglected, including how you feel about your parents.

■ Sometimes when hard things happen in life, people become stronger. How have the hard things in your life affected you?

CHAPTER 6

Abusive Behavior by Peers

Mistreatment or abusive behavior by peers is not legally called "abuse," but some of the behaviors are very similar to what we've discussed already about emotional, physical, or sexual abuse. Many of the behaviors are the same as those legally defined as abuse committed by an adult or caretaker—getting hit, being called names, being ignored, getting teased. Because the legal definition is not the same, the consequences differ for teens, but the behavior is still unacceptable—no matter what it's called. In this chapter, we'll use the words mistreatment or abusive behavior to describe intimidating, injurious, or insulting actions perpetrated by peers.

Abuse or mistreatment from other teens or someone close to your age often happens in dating and social relationships, at school, or in your own family. Abusive behavior or harassment can involve sexual, physical, or emotional actions. It may be that your boyfriend or girlfriend is being controlling or is physically pushing you around. Maybe some of the other kids at school are singling you out and giving you a hard time. Perhaps someone you're dating has even raped you. These are all examples of abusive behavior by peers.

These behaviors don't fit the criteria for child abuse discussed in this book, because the abuser isn't in a position of authority or control over you. Yet the behavior of other teens can still intimidate you and make you feel bad about yourself. Some of this behavior can also be considered assault in the eyes of the law. They're all examples of someone mistreating you.

What Is Bullying?
Bullying includes physical, emotional, verbal, and psychological behaviors. Physical aspects include hitting or pushing. Emotional

51

bullying includes making fun of you. Verbal bullying includes name-calling, and psychological behaviors include intimidating or scaring you. You can be bullied by one person or by a group. Being bullied can make you feel:

■ bad about yourself

■ scared

■ uncertain about being confronted or attacked

It may interfere with your schoolwork or even make you unable to sleep if you're constantly worrying about the bully.

About one-third of students are bullied at one time or another, most often in middle school. The climate, or environment, at your school can affect how much

Harassment

Harassment is more like emotional abuse than sexual or physical abuse. Harassment often involves sexual talk, jokes, or references, but not a sexual act. Harassment may also include bullying with words and physical intimidation, but again, doesn't usually end up in a physical exchange. Harassment can happen with people your own age or older, and often refers to things that are happening at school or at work.

There are guidelines—usually called grievance procedures—that protect workers and students from this type of treatment. Ask a teacher or supervisor about how to file a complaint at your school or workplace. Because harassment is an attacking form of behavior, it can make you feel scared, angry, or helpless. Don't try to handle harassment alone. Ask for help.

bullying happens there. Part of a school's climate includes how people at the school and in the community feel about bullying and violence. In a recent study, 40 percent of middle school and high school boys said they thought hitting or threatening is acceptable if someone makes them angry; 20 percent of girls agreed.[1] Those feelings make bullying more acceptable to these individuals. Teachers, principals, and counselors can help change the climate at school to a more positive one where bullying is not as acceptable.

Bullying May Look Like . . .

- Name-calling

- Personal verbal attacks (for example, against your clothes, the color of your skin, your friends or family, where you live, your religious beliefs, or your sexual orientation)

- Physical or verbal behaviors that intimidate or scare you (for example, shoving you in the hallway, glaring at you, pushing your books off your desk, spilling your soda or lunch tray)

- Snickering, laughing, or making gross noises when you talk in class or walk by

- Tripping you on the bus, in the hall, or in class

- Threatening you

- Taking money or your things

- Pressuring you to do their homework, chores, or anything else

Although bullying isn't considered abuse by the law, it often calls for intervention by parents, teachers, or others in authority. Yet adults often respond to bullying by suggesting that you "just ignore it" or "joke with them." These strategies aren't always effective. Ignoring the behavior may stop it eventually, but many teens feel frustrated and powerless when they follow this type of advice. What's more, teens don't feel understood or protected when they're given this advice by parents or teachers. Another common solution from adults, particularly within families, is to "work it out amongst yourselves." This can be frustrating too, because you probably would have already done that if you could.

For some reason, many adults believe that conflict with people your own age just isn't that traumatic. Yet the results for you can be truly devastating. Bullying can lead to significant problems; some teens become depressed or anxious as a result of others teasing them, being left out or isolated from peers, and from more extreme types of abuse. School shootings and other violence has also been linked to bullying. Teens who commit these violent attacks are often feeling isolated, left out, or misunderstood. Sometimes out of desperation, teens take matters of bullying into their own hands and take action on their own. These poor decisions can have deadly results.

Many of the feelings people have about being bullied are very much like the feelings people have from being abused in other ways. Bullies may use intimidation, which is another form of emotional abuse, in addition to the physical ways they attempt to control others. One major difference between abuse and bullying is that bullying is often more public than abuse. Being a bully can sometimes make the bully feel more powerful and popular with peers. This is really hard stuff because if nobody tells the bully it's wrong or bothers to help you out, you feel even more alone and worthless. What else can you assume if nobody speaks up to help? But others are probably feeling intimidated, too.

The advice that parents and adults often give about bullies—just ignore them—is partly why nobody may help you during a bullying incident. Even though this isn't okay—that nobody's helping—it may help to understand what's going on. The lack of help from others doesn't mean everyone else is against you. They just may be confused about what to do or they may be afraid the bully will attack them if they do speak up.

Some people who bully others are attempting to make themselves feel better in a warped way. Many times, bullies have suffered from abuse themselves. Knowing this doesn't excuse their behavior—but it might help you understand, so you feel less scared and take their attacks less personally. It's really not about you; it's about how they feel about themselves.

> I'm not so bad to everybody. But when they make me mad—I've got to do something. If someone hits me, I go off. I don't start it. He was sitting in my seat. All I did was push him.
>
> —JACOBI, 15

Seek out support from others. Even if adults around you (or your peers) don't give you support for trying to take care of yourself, don't give up on yourself. Keep looking for someone who will understand and help. Talk to your school counselor, a youth worker, or someone in your community whose job is to help teens, or check out some of the resources listed on pages 77–80.

People to include in your support network if you experience bullying

- You!—the more positive you feel about yourself, the easier it will be to speak up for yourself. As you grow in self-respect, you will become less of a target for bullies.

- Your friends—ask your friends to help you out. In a group, you're less likely to be bullied.

- Your parents or other trusted adults—even though you're trying to become independent, everybody needs help from others at times. Many times they'll respect you for asking, and who knows, you might even feel better about yourself, too.

- Counselors are available at several national hotlines, listed in the resources on pages 77–78. They can be another resource—to listen, to problem-solve, or just for support.

Remind yourself:
"I deserve to be treated with respect. I'll start with respecting myself."

Sometimes it can help you feel stronger about your choice to speak up and ask for assistance if you know that your actions will help someone else from being picked on this way, too. So, if you're not willing to stand up for yourself, how about for someone else? It might make you feel better.

What Is Date Rape?

Being raped on a date happens more frequently than most people realize. The percentage increases if drinking or drugs are used during the date. Experts estimate that between 10 and 25 percent of girls under age 18 are the victims of rape or attempted rape while in a dating relationship. Statistics about boys are harder to find because boys don't usually talk about or report date rape—they feel embarrassed, ashamed, and sometimes question their sexuality. Abuse can happen in either a gay or heterosexual (straight) relationship.

Often, date rape isn't reported because people may feel partially responsible because they chose to spend time alone with that person. Date rape can happen if you've been seeing someone for a while and even if you've had sex with the person before. Just because you said "yes" once doesn't mean the answer is always "yes." It's even okay to change your mind once you've started kissing or getting intimate. Once you say "no," the person needs to stop and respect your wishes.

People who might rape on a date also use "tricks," just like abusers we've talked about before. These tricks will usually be ways to try and make you feel guilty—like you "owe" them something at the end of a nice date. Maybe they will try to intimidate you into having sex by suggesting that it's the only way they can be sure you really care about them. There are many other ways of showing someone that you care about them. It may be hard, at first, to resist the other person because you're learning how to trust yourself, but you're beginning to make positive changes in your life—they don't have to happen all at once.

But sometimes when you say no, they won't stop. Some people may go on to commit date rape. They believe their feelings and desires are more important than yours. Some people believe it's okay to threaten or scare others to get their way. People who rape or abuse others often don't know other ways of getting what they want. They often don't know how to tell other people how they really feel. For example, they might like someone and not know how to tell them. That doesn't make it okay to just take what they want without caring about the other person. Maybe they don't understand what healthy relationships look like; they don't know or care about other people's feelings. Protecting yourself by not being alone with them, or maybe even not being around them, might be important ways for you to take care of yourself.

After a date rape, many people feel ashamed about what happened. They may blame themselves, kind of like what happens in sexual abuse. These kinds of feelings make it hard to talk about date rape, just like it is hard to talk about sexual abuse. Find someone close to you—friends, parents, or other adults—to talk to about the rape, and maybe then you can feel strong enough to report it.

If date rape has happened to you, your options are similar to those of someone who has been raped or assaulted by a stranger. You can turn to the police, which might involve going to court for you and could mean fines or jail time for the person who assaulted you. But what's most important is to take care of yourself. Get medical attention and ask for help from your social support network and the authorities. Taking care of yourself will involve talking to others about what happened and gaining support as you try to understand how someone you trusted and cared about could treat you this way.

Sometimes people who bully or sexually abuse others have grown up in homes where violence is accepted. This can be part of the reason they don't understand their behavior is not okay. It's not your job to teach them about what is okay—you just need to be able to take care of yourself.

> I dated Todd for a couple of years, and he wanted to have sex. I said "no," but we had been drinking that night, and I guess I just kind of passed out. I woke up the next morning and my head really hurt. My pants were on backwards, so I knew something had happened.
>
> —Emily, 16

What Is Relationship Abuse?

Other kinds of abuse or mistreatment can happen in close or dating relationships, including physical or emotional abuse. Here are some examples:

- jealous or controlling behavior
- name-calling
- getting angry when you aren't immediately available

- talking about all the things you do wrong
- humiliating you in front of other people
- flirting with other people in front of you
- lying about dating other people
- making you feel like you don't matter
- isolating you from family and friends

When you're being treated this way, you're more likely to choose other unhealthy behaviors in an attempt to feel better—like drinking, using other drugs, smoking, attempting suicide, or eating in unhealthy patterns. Emotional abuse in dating relationships often makes it hard for teens to figure out how to think for themselves. Unhealthy relationships can foster more abusive behavior and make the victim feel worse about themselves, but you don't have to feel stuck there. It may even take a while for you to decide if you are in an unhealthy relationship. Your friends or your parents may say something to you before you even notice, and that will probably just make you mad. But stay open to people who really care about you. They'll be there to help when you're ready to ask.

Remind yourself:
"I'm learning to feel good enough about myself that I won't stay in a relationship where I'm abused."

Being abused by someone you're dating—someone who's supposed to care about you—is just as confusing as being abused by an adult you trusted. If what's happening in the relationship makes you feel uncomfortable, find some other people to help you take care of yourself—friends, family, or other people in your support network.

***

Give yourself permission to ask for help. If something is happening to you in your dating relationship that makes you feel bad, stop and think about how it really makes you feel. Sometimes these abusive activities may have much milder labels, like teasing or being mean, but they still make you feel bad. Regardless of what you call them, the first step is just like that outlined in Chapter 1—recognizing it as abusive behavior so you can begin to develop a plan of action to take care of yourself.

Let It Out

Remember, writing in a journal is a great way to help you figure exactly what's going on in your life and how you feel about it. It's private and usually feels like a safer place to start than talking to someone face-to-face. It's okay if you don't feel ready to do any journaling. Respect yourself and your own pace. Just do those things that you feel ready to do.

- Write a plan to help stop bullying at your school.

- What was unhealthy about some of the relationships you've been in?

- Describe what a healthy relationship might look like for you. Make a list if that's easier.

CHAPTER 7

What If . . . ?

If you've been abused, you probably have lots of questions, some that are pretty specific. This chapter is about answering some of those questions.

What if I'm a boy who has been sexually abused by a man? Does this mean I'm gay?

This is a really common—and hard—question for boys. Just because you've been sexually abused by a man doesn't mean you're gay. You didn't choose to have sexual contact with another male—the abuser was the one making the decisions. What you experienced was an attack. You weren't choosing to have this happen to you. An attacker's actions, even if they include some sexual activity, can't turn you into a gay person. If you are gay, it's not because someone abused you.

What if I'm a girl who has been raped? What does it mean if I've lost my virginity in this way?

Giving up your virginity is a choice—something you give to someone you love. A rape is an attack over which you had no control. Because you had no choice, you didn't lose your virginity. Although you may experience physical signs similar to those of someone who has chosen to have sex for the first time, it's important to remember that you had no choice about this attack.

Remind yourself:
"I had no control over the rape."

What if someone in my family has sexually abused me? What does it mean to be involved in incest? What does this say about me?

Incest is especially hard because it makes you wonder about your family and yourself. Chances are that if you were sexually abused by someone in your family, the pattern of abuse had been in your family long before you were born. Sexual abuse that happens in families is especially confusing because families are supposed to love and protect you. You probably have mixed feelings about the person who abused you—some positive, some negative. That's a normal part of incest—having mixed feelings. Some people have a hard time understanding how you can care about someone who abused you, but that person who abused you is still part of your family. You may love him or her or have warm feelings toward the person simply because you are in the same family. This is especially true if the abuser is a parent figure.

The abuser's bad decision doesn't say anything about you, except that you were a victim of the person's decisions and actions.

> My mom used to have me touch her when I was really little. It kept happening until my aunt found out a few years ago—it felt weird, but I didn't know it wasn't okay. I thought everybody did it. I don't talk to very many people about it now, but I'm feeling better about it because it stopped.
>
> —MIKE, 13

What if I'm a male? Can I be raped?

Males can be raped by either a male or female. Males are more likely to be victims of forcible sodomy (anal rape) by another male—59 percent of male victims are under age 18. Most authorities agree that the statistics for males are very underreported. Embarrassment and questioning one's own sexuality are common reasons men and boys don't report being raped or sodomized. Our culture also promotes sexuality, almost as a rite of passage for boys—making it seem like having sex is cool, no matter who it's with. This is another reason males often don't report being raped or abused.

What if my mom or dad abused me?

Your feelings may be even stronger and more confusing if you were abused by a parent. Parents are supposed to take care of you and protect you. When one of them abuses you, it shatters your expectations about their role in your life. That can be one of the hardest parts of the abuse for you. It can make it hard to trust anyone. Some teens even wonder if they'll ever be able to be in a relationship or have kids, because they're afraid they'll abuse their own children, as they were abused. These fears are normal. But just because you were abused doesn't mean that you have to or will abuse others. Even if people in your family have abused others a lot, that doesn't have to be something you carry on. Getting help and talking with others will make it easier for you to stop a cycle of abuse if it exists in your family.

> It makes me sad my own dad doing this. I cry about how my life is so different now since my dad started abusing me.
>
> —Ann, 15

Some teens also feel embarrassed about what their parents have done, but you can't control what other people do—even your parents. It was their decision to abuse you—you have no responsibility for that decision and no reason to feel guilty about or responsible for the abuse. That can be a difficult place to get to, but the sooner you believe that it wasn't your fault, the better you'll feel. It may help to talk to somebody else about how you feel.

Your relationship with your parents will continue in some way—they'll always be your parents, no matter what they've done. Although you don't have a choice about them being your parents, you do have choices about how you want that relationship to be now. It's okay to set up boundaries, even with parents.

What if my brother or sister abused me?

Abuse from a brother or sister can be different from other kinds of abuse. Sibling relationships are unique. How close you feel to your brother or sister will affect how you think, act, and feel about the abuse. If you feel close, your sibling will probably use that closeness to keep you from talking about what's happened. If you don't feel as close, your (usually older) sibling will try to intimidate you into participating and keeping quiet. Siblings can have a way of making you feel more responsible for the abuse, when you're not. A brother or sister can make you feel afraid that parents will blame you for the abuse, and that can keep you from telling.

Other emotional reactions resulting from sibling abuse also depend on the quality of the relationship with your brother or sister. In a closer relationship, you may have less extreme emotional reactions, because you may be more forgiving toward your sibling. However, you may feel more angry and betrayed, too. Part of this depends on how much you feel your sibling took advantage of you. In a more distant sibling relationship, your feelings and reactions usually depend on how intimidated you may feel.

Again, what's important to remember is that the decision about the abuse was not yours—it was that of your sibling, no matter how much he or she tries to make you believe otherwise.

What if I chose to have sex with my brother or sister?

Sometimes siblings "experiment" in sexual ways with each other because they feel close to each other. Experimentation is not the same as having sex. Having sex with a sibling, however, is incest—whether it's intercourse, oral sex, or some other kind of penetration. Having sex with a brother or sister is not part of a healthy sibling relationship. Counseling is usually part of what happens after this kind of sexual contact is reported. If the sexual contact is severe, however, a temporary change in living arrangements—like having your sibling live elsewhere—may be recommended.

What if the abuser was drunk or high?

Many people tend to "let the abuser off" or don't hold the person as responsible if the abuser was drinking or using drugs during the abuse. Although drug use can impair judgment, it doesn't absolve (clear or free) the abuser of responsibility. The abuser still chose his or her actions. If the abuser was drinking or using other drugs, he or she may remember fewer details about the abuse, but that doesn't change the fact that you were hurt and that it was abuse.

Remind yourself:
"The abuser is always responsible for what happened."

What if I was drunk or high when the abuse occurred?

Drinking or getting high puts anyone at greater risk for being abused. You're much less able to take care of yourself by following through after you've said "no." If you're drunk or high, you may be even less aware of the abuse actually happening. Many sexual abusers want you to drink or get high because then you're much more vulnerable and likely to let them do what they want. It's important to remember, however, that it's still abuse, even if you were under the influence of alcohol or other drugs.

What if the sexual abuse felt good in some ways?

Our bodies are wired or designed to feel good when touched in certain ways. That doesn't mean you "liked" the abuse or wanted it to continue. It simply means that's the way our bodies are put together. Sexual touching often does feel good—this is to make sure more people are created. It has a biological basis to further the species. You can't fight that much evolution or biological history.

What if I've been abused by someone in my church, synagogue, or other religious place?

One of the difficult things about this kind of abuse is how others see the abuser. Religious leaders are respected by adult members of the congregation, making it even harder for you to speak up. As with abuse by a family member, you may have positive and negative feelings about someone in the church, synagogue, or mosque who abuses you. Unfortunately, the authority from their position is usually a large part of the control they have over you. Finding someone who will listen to you may be a challenge, but you'll find the support you need. Think about the people you trust and talk to them about what happened.

What if it was a teacher or coach who abused me in some way? What if I consented to sex with my teacher?

Abuse by a teacher or coach is similar to abuse by other authority figures. However, you may feel more of a friendship with an adult who's part of your daily life. You may admire many things about your teacher or coach and feel special if this person pays extra attention to you. Even though you may have mixed feelings about having sex with a teacher or a coach, your admiration for this person and desire to be closer or "special" may push you to have sex with him or her.

Even if you've "consented" and feel you're old enough to make a decision about having sex with a teacher or a coach, or anyone for that matter, by law you're considered too young to give consent if you're under age 18. When an adult has sex with an underage person, it's called "statutory rape," and despite your "consent," charges may be brought against the teacher or coach. The "power differential" in the relationship puts you at risk, regardless of the legal issues. A power differential means the abuser is in charge. They have power over you. They may have power because they're older, because they're threatening to hurt you or someone else, or just because they make it hard for you to trust yourself. Whatever the reason, the power differential is something that makes it hard for you to say no or to talk to someone else about the abuse.

What if I was abused by someone my own age? Can bullying be considered abuse?

Someone your own age can be abusive toward you, whether it involves sexual, physical, or emotional behaviors. Bullying is often similar to emotional abuse (such as name-calling) and sometimes physical abuse (such as pushing or shoving). Although another teen doesn't have any official authority or control over you, his or her behavior can still intimidate you and leave you feeling bad about yourself. (See Chapter 6 for more on bullying.)

What if I caused the abuse, maybe I'm partly to blame?

The abuser wants you to feel that you're to blame. But there's nothing you could have done to "cause" the abuse. It doesn't matter how you dressed or if you were drinking yourself—you didn't cause the abuse. You may have even said "no," and the abuse still happened. The abuser is responsible for his or her actions and probably intimidated, forced, or coerced you to get you to participate.

What if I've been abusive toward others?

Sometimes people who have been abused will abuse others, but that doesn't always happen. Even if you have abused others, you can choose to stop, although you'll probably need help to do so. Lots of people who've been abused try to go on without thinking about what's happened to them or by blocking out the pain of the abuse. Stopping your own abusive behavior means you'll have to deal with your feelings about your own experience of being abused. Some people who abuse others are unaware that they've been abused themselves. The behavior of abusing others is often a way your body communicates or telegraphs that you've been abused. You can find other ways to release your feelings related to the abuse. As a place to start, you can brainstorm ideas on your own, but abuse makes life complicated, so finding a professional to help you is a very good idea.

> ### Remind yourself:
> "I can choose to stop my behavior."

What if I've been abused by someone I met in a chatroom? The person pretended to be someone he or she wasn't.

Chatrooms are potentially very dangerous. In these settings, adults often pretend to be teens, especially those who want to abuse children and teens. It's a bad idea to give out personal information or meet someone in person who you've met online. It can be tempting to do so when you're sharing your feelings with someone online, but there are many "predators" on the Internet. The person may take advantage of you. If you were abused by someone you met in a chatroom, tell someone—a teacher, your DARE officer at school, a scout leader or coach, or your parents. You may have known that what you were doing was risky and are now afraid of getting in trouble, but those around you want you to be safe. If you're in trouble, they want to help. If you're 20 miles from home or 200 miles from home meeting this person, call for help—it's never too late. If you haven't met this person yet, don't!

What if the abuse has been happening in my family for so long that it's all that I've ever known?

If abuse is all you've ever known, change will be challenging. Making a change will feel weird or different at first, but those feelings of something being different can help you make a change. Once you realize that change will feel weird, you can begin to accept that feeling and know it means something good instead of something bad. This may even be a way to begin trusting your feelings. Then get help from an adult outside the family—someone you're sure you can trust.

What if the physical abuse has left me permanently disabled?

If the abuse has left you with a permanent disability, your struggle to heal will be challenging on many levels. You'll need to focus on rehabilitation or adjustment to the physical changes in your life, which may involve changing your image of yourself as well as your activity level. You'll also need to focus on healing from the abuse. The severity of the abuse will affect your healing process. If your physical changes are serious and change the way you live—for example, there are certain sports or activities you can no longer do as a result of the abuse—your adjustment will probably be more challenging. You'll probably have stronger feelings about the abuse and may be more angry or sad as well. Big changes (whether good or bad) are always stressful. You'll have to deal with the immediate stress of the change and the longer adjustment to not being able to do certain things. Part of your recovery will include grieving for the abilities you've lost.

What if the abuse is considered normal in my family or my culture?

If abuse is considered "normal," this book and other sources are even more important to help you move forward in your life. When everyone around you believes that something is okay, but you don't, you may have more of a struggle to find support—but you can find it. In these cases, the Internet or other resources may be a good place to look for support. But, be cautious about predators on the Internet. Sometimes chat rooms may feel so friendly it's easy to assume they're safe, but some of those people who say they're teenagers really aren't and some adults who offer help may not really want to help you. See the resources listed at the end of each Part for suggestions on where to start.

***

There are lots of questions about abuse. I hope some of yours have been answered in this chapter, and you feel better by learning you're not alone with your experiences and your questions. Knowing that others have similar feelings or thoughts can help you feel better about deciding what to do for yourself. Lots of people have survived abuse and found a way to get the support they need. You can do that, too. You have the strength to ask others for the support you need.

Let It Out

Remember, writing in a journal is a great way to help you figure exactly what's going on in your life and how you feel about it. It's private and usually feels like a safer place to start than talking to someone face-to-face. It's okay if you don't feel ready to do any journaling. Respect yourself and your own pace. Just do those things that you feel ready to do.

- List the ways you feel less alone after reading this chapter.

- What did you learn in this chapter that has helped you feel stronger and better about yourself?

CHAPTER 8

It's Not Your Fault

Embracing the fact that the abuse wasn't your fault is one of the most important lessons you can take away from this book. You may have been told this message already, and I hope you believe it. It's often hard to believe that the abuse wasn't your fault because the abuser wanted you to believe that. Don't let that person control you by continuing to believe on any level that the abuse was your fault. It wasn't. The abuser made the decisions and pressured you not to tell. The abuser did this to you—when something bad happens to you, it's not your fault.

Whose Fault Is It?

Abuse is always the fault of the abuser. Although this person will use tricks, force, and fear tactics to make you believe you're partly to blame, you're not. We all have a need to feel in control of our lives, but as much as you might like to believe otherwise, the abuser has been in control and has made the decisions about the abuse. Did you choose to get hit, touched sexually, or called names? No, of course not. You probably looked for ways to make these things not happen—like being away from the house, staying in your room to avoid contact, or giving in to what they wanted. Those were survival strategies for you. You chose to survive and looked for ways to make that happen. Choices about how to survive the abuse have been yours, but the abuse was not.

Why Do You Feel Like You've Done Something Wrong?

Many times, people who abuse want you to feel bad about what's going on, so you won't tell. Again, the abuser wants you to feel partly responsible, so you'll be afraid of getting in trouble, too. It may be difficult to think about the person who abused you being so mean, tricky, and deceitful, but part of this person is that way, or the abuse wouldn't have happened in the first place. When you think about the parts of the abuser that you may like, it's easier to doubt yourself because you may have a harder time believing the abuser is at fault. You may feel there are some nice things about this person—there may be—but don't let those "nice" parts cloud your judgment about what really happened. When someone does nice things and bad things, it can be very confusing and hard to figure out what's right. You did nothing wrong. Don't allow yourself to take the blame that belongs to the abuser.

Another way that people blame themselves and feel bad is by thinking that they somehow provoked or invited the abuse. You didn't. Many times in child and teen sexual abuse, the abuser actually teaches you how they want you to behave during the abuse. Sexual touch may even feel good. Our bodies are built to enjoy sexual feelings, and that can make the abuse seem confusing, or like it's your fault. The abuser may have taught you sexual behavior, but that doesn't mean it's your fault. If it feels good, that doesn't mean it's your fault. The role of an adult is to let you know what's right and wrong, not encourage you to make decisions and take action that's not in your best interest. Getting you to feel guilty about the abuse and to participate in it is in the best interest of the abuser, not you.

If there was physical or emotional abuse, you may feel you somehow provoked the person's anger and, therefore, partly blame yourself. How do you think you provoked the abuser? By spilling a glass of milk, by laughing or talking, by doing your homework and not getting some kind of chores done? These are normal things that happen in the life of a family, not reasons for abusing someone. Maybe you got angry about something and the abuser hit you. Everyone has a right to their feelings, including anger. That's not a reason to hit somebody else. If you got so angry that you tried to hit the adult, the adult's role is to help you calm down, not hit you back. Abusive behavior establishes abnormal ways of interacting and abnormal expectations. Don't let an abnormal or skewed way of thinking about your actions affect how you feel about yourself. Find a professional (if you can) who you can talk to about your experiences, someone who can help you understand what really happened.

Remind yourself:
"I will control how I feel about myself."

It doesn't matter if:

- alcohol or other drugs were used during the abuse
- the abuse felt kind of good to your body
- the abuser had you be abusive to someone else

None of these things make the abuse your fault. They are other kinds of "mind tricks" to push you toward feeling bad and guilty. Don't be tricked. You did nothing wrong.

My uncle touched me ever since I was little. I didn't like it, but I didn't have a daddy around, and he felt like a daddy to me. I think that's why it went on for so long. Mama thought it was good for me to be with Tyrone, and some things about it were good. He bought me nice things and took me to the zoo, like a daddy would. He just did the other things that I didn't know daddies don't do, at first. Then when I figured out this didn't happen with my friends' daddies, Tyrone made me feel like it was my fault it kept happening. He said he just did it to be nice to me, and he told me how I acted like I liked it, and I kinda guess I did. That made it go on even longer, 'cause I thought I would get in trouble for it, too. What finally helped me was when some girl came to school and talked about sexual abuse—she could have been me, and she didn't get in trouble when she talked about it. She talked to her home-school communicator—we've got one of those and she's pretty cool. I talked to her, and she helped me make it stop.

—Keisha, 17

How Do Abusers Lie?

Abusers tell lots of lies. They may lie to:

- get you in situations where they can abuse you
- convince you that what's happening isn't really abuse or even wrong
- make you keep the secret

Abusers are often good liars. When they tell you something again and again, sometimes you begin to believe them. They may manipulate you into feeling bad about yourself or scare you into not listening to yourself. In some ways that's the worst thing that happens when you're abused—you stop listening to and trusting yourself.

Lies About the Abuse

> That's all I remember because I passed out—I was drinking a lot. When I woke up, he was having sex with me and I told him to stop! He said, "You're dreaming—go back to sleep." He lied to me.
>
> —CYNTHIA, 16

People who abuse often use different tricks or ways of trying to make you think what's happening is normal, not abusive. They may say they wouldn't treat you this way if they didn't care. But that little voice inside you may be hinting that everything isn't okay and that the kinds of things that are happening aren't normal.

People who sexually abuse others often say the relationship is special or that this is how people show they care about each other. In any kind of abuse, they may scare you so much that you don't dare tell or even suggest that something is wrong. These are examples of the abuser trying to make you stop trusting your own view of reality—it's dangerous not being able to trust yourself. If you can't trust yourself, you can't protect yourself. You have to learn to trust yourself, and in cases of abuse, that's probably going to mean not doing what the abuser asks you to do. When you're being abused, it's not just okay to say no to adults or the abuser—you *need* to say no. It may feel uncomfortable at first, but this is one of those self-care behaviors you will need to practice. Trust your feelings about when it feels safe to start saying no—you may not feel ready to say no until you get help. That's okay, too. Do what you need to do when you are ready to do it.

Messages and Lies Used to Make You Think It's Not Abuse

- "This is our special relationship."

- "This is for your own good."

- "I'm just doing this because you're too stupid to figure things out for yourself."

- "You have to learn the hard way, just like I did."

- "It only hurts the first time."

- "I wouldn't do this if I didn't love you so much."

- "You have to help out. Your mom can't do anything right."

- "I'm the only one who keeps this family together."

- "You just fell down the stairs, remember?"

- "You think that hurt? Just you wait."

- "Don't whine—be a man."

Lies and Threats to Keep You Quiet

I couldn't do anything. If I screamed, I knew they would do something to me. I was scared to see what they would do 'cause I was already really scared. They already held my arms down and kept my mouth shut while they did it. Then they laughed about it while I sat on the floor and cried.

—Lynn, 16

The use of force or threats of violence are common during sexual or emotional abuse. Fear is a powerful tool for abusers that clouds your thinking and makes you question your own judgment.

Remind yourself:
"I will not be controlled by threats anymore."

Abusers may often make harmful threats against people you love to keep you involved in the abuse. If you've already shown the abuser that you may not care what he or she does to you, the person may begin to threaten those around you. Threatening to abuse a younger sibling or one of your cousins can be a really sneaky way to keep you involved. Because you care about the younger people in your family, you may "sacrifice" yourself by continuing to be abused so that they won't. You need to question how much you can believe the abuser's promise not to hurt others. This person has probably lied to you. Maybe a promise not to harm others for your silence is another lie. Abusers usually know you well enough to "personalize" their threats in the way that will scare you, hurt you, or intimidate you the most.

Threats about destroying your family are also used by abusers to control you. They may say that your family will fall apart or break up if you talk about abuse. Although

Things an Abuser May Say or Do to Make You Keep the Secret

"Nobody will believe you."

"It's your fault that you didn't tell anybody."

"I'll hurt you if you tell."

"Your mom will hate you if you tell."

"You won't get any more presents if you tell."

"Our family will fall apart and it'll be your fault if you tell."

"You know you liked it."

"I thought what we had was special."

"I never meant to hurt you."

"I never hit you—I only called you names—what a wimp."

your family may change after the abuse has been revealed, these changes will most likely be positive in the long-term—and they'll probably feel better than the continued abuse.

Another thing that happens a lot in abusive relationships is that abusers "forget" their behavior and they may apologize later. They may "forget" that they hit you or yelled at you. They may say they are really, really sorry and it'll never happen again. Abusers who apologize like this are often under the influence of alcohol or other drugs at the time of the abuse—which, again, doesn't excuse their behavior. You need to ask yourself how many times you've heard the abuser say those words, and how many times the abuse has happened again. Even if the abuse just happens once, and even if the abuser apologizes, it doesn't make the abuse go away. When someone apologizes and promises to end the abuse, it can make you question yourself, too. That's one of the main ways that abusers keep you from talking—by making you question yourself.

When abusers lie to you, they have one major goal: They're trying to get you to stop believing your inner voice—that's an extremely dangerous thing for you to do, yet it can happen very easily. It's often easier to listen to others instead of yourself, because it may seem like there will be less conflict. Less conflict may not be worth that part of yourself you have to give up.

Trust Your Inner Voice

An important part of healing that can happen on your own or in counseling or therapy, is to reconnect with or discover your inner voice, to learn to trust yourself and your judgment again—or for the very first time.

Remind yourself:
"I'm listening to my inner voice to make decisions."

You may not know what it feels like to listen to an "inner voice." You can begin by thinking about your conscience—your sense of right and wrong is part of your inner voice. An inner voice or a conscience usually makes itself known in very subtle ways—

an uncomfortable feeling, like a feeling of dread or doom about something, or a feeling of nervousness or anxiousness, just feeling like something's not right. Think back to a time when you were faced with a choice about doing something right or wrong. When people are dealing with these types of decisions, they often experience a little internal twinge—a feeling that something wasn't quite right. That's an inner voice. It takes practice to get used to listening to that voice, but you can do it.

***

It may feel like a lot of work so far, but I hope you've been able to clarify some of your feelings and thoughts about what's happening in your life. Knowing that others have experienced some of the same types of things can give you strength and a different way of looking at things—a way to feel empowered and tuned in to yourself. Knowing what feels right to you can be a new experience as well. It may take a little time to feel confident about your own views on things. Sorting out your feelings helps you feel more in control. Having labels for abuse can give you tools to talk with others about your experiences. Talking about your experiences—asking for help—is an important step in your healing process. The next part of the book will help you get started.

Let It Out

Remember, writing in a journal is a great way to help you figure exactly what's going on in your life and how you feel about it. It's private and usually feels like a safer place to start than talking to someone face-to-face. It's okay if you don't feel ready to do any journaling. Respect yourself and your own pace. Just do those things that you feel ready to do.

■ Describe why the abuse isn't your fault.

■ What lies were you told?

Resources

Hotlines

Childhelp USA's National Child Abuse Hotline
1-800-4-A-CHILD (1-800-422-4453)
For more information about Childhelp USA and their national hotline, see page 80.

Covenant House Nineline—Crisis Intervention Hotline
1-800-999-9999
www.covenanthouse.org
This hotline is available 24 hours a day and provides immediate crisis intervention for youth in any kind of dangerous or difficult situation. Call for advice, support, or referrals to resources where you can get the help you need. You can also visit their Web site to learn about their nationwide youth programs or to read more information about abuse, suicide, running away, substance abuse, and other problems.

Kids Help Phone Counseling Service
1-800-668-6868
www.kidshelp.sympatico.ca
Kids Help Phone is a 24-hour counseling service for Canadian youth. Services are confidential and provided both in English and French. Call about anything from problems at home or school to substance abuse, sexuality issues, or suicide.

National Domestic Violence Hotline
1-800-799-SAFE (1-800-799-7233)
www.ndvh.org
This 24-hour hotline offers crisis intervention, educational materials, and referrals to local shelters and other services that are available to domestic violence victims and their families. Their Web site also offers useful information and practical suggestions for staying safe.

National Hopeline Network—Suicide Prevention Hotline
1-800-SUICIDE (1-800-784-2433)
www.hopeline.com
This 24-hour hotline connects you to the nearest crisis center where counseling and mental health care referrals are available. Visit their Web site to find links to other depression and suicide resources.

National Hotline for Missing and Exploited Children
1-800-THE-LOST (1-800-843-5678)
www.missingkids.com
This 24-hour hotline is available for reporting the abduction or maltreatment of children. In close contact with law enforcement officials, operators can help you stay safe or aid in the search for a friend or loved one. Their Web site is a great source of statistics about abuse and maltreatment as well as information for staying safe on the Internet.

National Sexual Assault Hotline
1-800-656-HOPE (1-800-656-4673)
See page 80 for more information about this hotline and the Rape, Abuse & Incest National Network (RAINN), the organization that operates it.

Books

But He Says He Loves Me: Girls Speak Out on Dating Abuse by Nicole B. Sperekas (Brandon, VT: Safer Society Foundation, 1998). Read about the experiences of girls who have suffered all forms of dating abuse (verbal, emotional, physical, and sexual), and learn how to protect yourself from becoming a victim.

Child Abuse by Edward F. Dolan (New York: Franklin Watts, 1992). Read about physical and sexual abuse, neglect, incest, and child pornography. Real-life examples and study results outline the severity of abuse, practical strategies offer tips for staying safe, and resources lead the way to more support.

Drugs and Domestic Violence by Raymond M. Jamiolkowski (New York: Rosen Publishing Group, 1996). This book explores the link between drugs and violence in the home. Learn why drugs can worsen domestic violence, the toll substance abuse can have on families, and practical ways to escape a very dangerous situation.

Family Abuse: A National Epidemic by Maria Hong (Springfield, NJ: Enslow Publishers, 1997). Learn about the different types of family abuse, the impact of abuse on victims, and patterns and risk factors for each type of abuse. Resources point the way to help if you are a victim or in danger of being abused.

Katie.com: My Story by Katherine Tarbox (New York: Penguin, 2001). This is the true story of a 13-year-old girl who is estranged from her family and finds comfort when she meets "Mark" in a chat room on the Internet. Mark, a 41-year-old man, poses as a 23-year-old college student and uses their online relationship to manipulate Katie into meeting, eventually sexually abusing her. This account of abuse is a startling instance of the potential dangers of the Internet.

Web Sites

Bullying Online
www.bullying.co.uk
Being bullied at school takes away from learning and makes school a miserable experience. This site offers you help and advice for dealing with bullies.

Love Doesn't Have to Hurt Teens
www.apa.org/pi/pii/teen
Developed by the American Psychological Association, this site offers information about dating violence in teen relationships. Determine whether you are a victim, discover how to help abused friends, and find out where to go for support.

National Exchange Club Foundation
www.preventchildabuse.com
Committed to the prevention of child abuse, this organization's Web site is a great source of information for abuse, national programs, and contact information for abuse organizations.

Prevent Child Abuse Now
www.prevent-abuse-now.com
This site offers comprehensive information about abuse and related topics. Find articles, statistics, and tips for staying safe. Survivor poetry, victim services, and a listing of resources is also available, with links to organizations that want to help.

Safe Child
www.safechild.org
While also for parents and teachers, this site offers great information on bullying, child abuse, violence prevention, and Internet safety.

Safe Teens
www.safeteens.com
The World Wide Web is an exciting and informative place. Unfortunately, it also carries its share of risks. This site offers all of the information that you need to surf the Web while staying safe and protecting your privacy.

Organizations

American Association of Suicidology
4201 Connecticut Avenue NW, Suite 408
Washington, DC 20008
(202) 237-2280
www.suicidology.org
This organization is dedicated to the study and prevention of suicide. They provide accurate and in-depth information about suicide, a referral service for local crisis centers and support groups, and links and resources for depressed individuals. The number listed above is not a crisis line; callers in crisis should dial 1-800-784-2433.

Childhelp USA
15757 North 78th Street
Scottsdale, AZ 85260
1-800-4-A-CHILD (1-800-422-4453)
www.childhelpusa.org
This national organization offers treatment programs and provides temporary or permanent homes for severely abused youth. Their hotline, listed above, is staffed 24 hours a day and features professional counselors that can direct you to emergency and support services located in your area.

National Clearinghouse on Child Abuse and Neglect
330 C Street SW
Washington, DC 20447
1-800-394-3366
www.calib.com/nccanch
This government agency offers the nation's largest database of information about abuse and neglect. Call the toll-free automated phone number, write, or visit their Web site for statistics about abuse, tips for preventing and stopping abuse, and a summary of legal issues involved. Also available on the Web site is a listing of toll-free numbers for reporting abuse in individual states; it's located at *www.calib.com/nccanch/pubs/prevenres/organizations/tollfree.cfm*. Please note that not all states have toll-free numbers for reporting abuse. In the case that yours does not, call 1-800-422-4453.

National Council on Child Abuse & Family Violence (NCCAFV)
1025 Connecticut Avenue NW, Suite 1012
Washington, DC 20036
www.nccafv.org
This organization provides information about child and domestic abuse. Write or visit their Web site for information on all of the forms that abuse takes and methods for preventing it.

Rape, Abuse & Incest National Network
635-B Pennsylvania Avenue SE
Washington, DC 20003
1-800-656-HOPE (1-800-656-4673)
www.rainn.org
The nation's largest anti-sexual assault organization, RAINN provides information about sexual assault to the public. Their national hotline, listed above, connects callers to the nearest rape crisis center for counseling and support services.

Part 2

2

Taking

Action

CHAPTER 9

Getting Safe

The first part of this book focused on figuring out what's going on—giving names to behaviors. Understanding your experience is sometimes necessary before you can take action or make a change. You've also been exploring the possibility of doing something differently in your life. Bill O'Hanlon, a therapist who has written about abuse and many other subjects, suggests that each of us can "do one thing differently" no matter what's happening in our lives. What is that one thing you would choose to do differently? Reading this book may be the first thing you've chosen to do differently. What's next for you? Choosing to do one thing differently can be a step toward getting safe.

> **Remind yourself:**
> "I can do one thing differently."

How Can You Say "No"?

Maybe one of the things you'll choose to do differently is to think about saying "no." This may not be something you feel safe doing because you're worried about the abuser getting more mad at you and hurting you or someone else you love. If that's how you feel, trust those feelings. But if you think it might be safe to say "no," begin practicing—in front of the mirror, to a friend, to your dog, or in your mind. Practicing with someone else can help you feel less alone or scared about taking this step. You may even want to have someone with you when you say "no" to the abuser. You don't have to do any of these hard things by yourself anymore.

Here are some ways to say "no":

- "No!"

- "Stop hurting me."

- "Leave me alone."
- "It's not okay for you to . . ."
- "You've lied to me."
- "I don't like what you're doing to me."
- "This isn't how you show somebody you care."
- "I don't want you to do this to me anymore."

How Do You Get Safe Right Now?

Being abused is frightening. It makes you feel unsafe, perhaps even in your own home. At times, you may have wondered if the abuse would ever stop or if there's anything else you could try to make it stop. Feeling stuck in that way can make you feel like nobody cares, like you're all alone, or even lost and hopeless. I hope you're not in that place right now, but if you are, please know that there are people who care about you and who can help. Together, with people who care about you—people who are probably already part of your daily life—you can stop the abuse and the awful pain you've been feeling. Hang in there, reach out for support, and someone will help you find a way out of your pain. You're not alone, even though it may feel that way for now.

If you need *immediate* help, call a child abuse hotline or the police.

Abuse Hotlines

Most states have "800" (free) phone numbers to report abuse, or a local phone number in your county to call. These are usually found under the government listings in your phone book or under Child Abuse Hotline or Family/Social Services. A Web site that lists phone numbers for each state can be found on page 80. The national number is 1-800-422-4453.

Anyone can call the hotline, so if you want to report the abuse yourself, go ahead and call. Although you can also contact the police directly, the hotline is a free phone call just for child abuse. When you call, the hotline counselor will need to know basic identifying information about you—age, address, and details about the abuse and the abuser. Within 24 to 48 hours of your call, someone from the agency will talk with you at

continued ➡

your school or home—if you're afraid to have the workers visit your home, tell them so. They can visit you at school and place you in a protected environment right away—usually an emergency foster placement if you don't have a safe place to go.

Calling the hotline may feel like a safer way to ask for help than confronting your abuser face-to-face, telling someone in your support network, or calling the police. That's one of the reasons the hotline is available—to make it easier for you and other people who want to help you to call.

My mama left me all alone that night. She went out and that's when I decided to call somebody. My friends are such big blabbermouths that they'd tell everybody, so I didn't want to tell them—and it was okay to call an 800 number 'cause there's no charge for that. The lady on the phone was really nice. She listened to me talk and asked a few questions. She didn't ask who I was, but she offered to call the police for me if I needed. I probably would have run away that night if I hadn't talked to her. I was getting so tired of Mama not doing anything to help me. I'm so mad at her! But now I've got some ideas about not getting so mad and what I can do to get help.

—Tasha, 13

Remind yourself:
"I feel strong enough to start getting safe."

How Do You Find Support?
Sometimes it may feel like you're all alone when you have to figure all this out for yourself.

Your support system is made up of all the resources available to you, including:

■ social networks—such as friends and family

■ community resources—such as teachers at school, coaches, scout leaders, or leaders of religious organizations

■ professionals, authorities, or agencies—such as therapists, police, and Child Protective Services

All these resources can help you in different ways during difficult times in your life. The support may be just to listen, or may be more active, like protecting you from abuse.

Make a list of people who could be—or already are—part of your support network, or team. Find the phone numbers of these people and write them on a small card you can carry with you in case of an emergency. Even having the list with you can feel comforting, as if you're ready for anything. Having a plan or an idea of what you intend to do can give you a sense of relief and empowerment. You can do this.

> It seemed like I was in a no-win situation, and there was no one to turn to.
>
> —PIERRE, 18

Some teens think about running away to escape the abuse in their homes. Although this may seem like a good solution, it may not be any better outside your home. It's very hard for teens to find jobs that pay well enough to support themselves. For this reason, many teens who run away end up using sex to make money, and they put themselves in even more abusive and frightening situations than they tried to leave. Using your support system is a much healthier way to get yourself out of an abusive home or family situation. Talking to the parent of a friend, a teacher, your school counselor, your DARE officer, or calling the child abuse hotline in your community are all ways to ask for help that are much safer than running away. It may seem romantic to run away and be on your own, but it's usually kind of scary. Many runaway teens end up living on the streets, having no regular place to bathe, no safe place to sleep, and no regular place to eat. People on the streets may seem friendly at first, but after you've known them a while, you may learn that they just want to make money from you having sex with other people.

If you've already run away from home, you can still get help. It's never too late. Covenant House is a group that helps runaway teens. They have a national toll-free hotline—Covenant House Nineline (1-800-999-9999).

***

I hope you're beginning to recognize your strengths and courage to make changes in your life. Doing one thing differently is something you can manage. You're worth the effort to make your life better. Other people will respect you more, too, when they see how well you are taking care of yourself.

Remind yourself:
"I can make a plan to take care of myself."

Let It Out

Remember, writing in a journal is a great way to help you figure exactly what's going on in your life and how you feel about it. It's private and usually feels like a safer place to start than talking to someone face-to-face. It's okay if you don't feel ready to do any journaling. Respect yourself and your own pace. Just do those things that you feel ready to do.

- For as many days as possible, choose one thing that you can do differently that day. Can you come up with a week's worth? How about a month? How much change are you ready for? Record these changes in your journal.

- Make a list of ways you're comfortable saying "no."

CHAPTER 10

Getting Ready to Tell

Telling others about the abuse, or even thinking about telling, can be very hard. You don't know what to expect; you may be scared; or you may have a lot of mixed-up feelings about what will happen once others know. That's normal. This chapter will look at what holds people back from telling and the positive effects of finally coming forward. Knowing that you're not alone in your fears and concerns is often helpful as you get ready to tell.

> I always thought talking about things made it worse—nobody talks in my family. But I felt a lot better after I talked to the school counselor.
>
> —AMY, 16

Why Don't People Tell?

People keep quiet about abuse for many different reasons, but some are commonly experienced. Knowing that other people have had similar feelings and experiences can help give you the courage to take action. Here are some common reasons why people don't tell and what you can do to get past them.

Fear and Threats

> I couldn't do anything because I was afraid they'd do something to me. I didn't want to see what else they would do.
>
> —TIFFANY, 16

87

Abuse can make you feel scared, especially if the abuse was violent. And if the abuser has threatened to hurt you—or someone you care about—if you tell, you probably still believe that (even if it's just a little bit deep inside you). It's normal to want to protect yourself from getting hurt again—that's a basic survival mechanism.

You may feel afraid and anxious to do anything about the abuse, including talking or journaling about it. You may even feel like the abuser knows what you're thinking or planning to do, even though you know this isn't possible. When you're scared or feeling controlled by someone else, you may not be thinking real clearly. Because of your fear or anger, you may not realize how much you're already being hurt. What have you got to lose by asking for help? You probably have more of yourself to lose by doing nothing than by talking. Since you know your situation better than anyone else, you can trust your own feelings about finding the safest way to ask for help.

Find someone you can really trust to help you feel protected—someone you can talk to about all the things you're afraid of that have kept you from telling before. Somebody else can help you understand that some of your fears may be irrational—many of the things you're afraid of won't happen. Fears and other feelings affect our thoughts and decisions. Sometimes it helps to have someone else help us figure out which fears are likely to happen and which aren't.

Remind yourself:
"I can take action to stop the abuse."

Family Patterns

Family patterns may make it hard for you to talk. All families have different expectations about handling sensitive subjects and may want things to remain hidden, including a history of abuse. You can find the patterns in your family on your own or with the help of family members or a therapist. It all depends on how close you feel with your family. Maybe it's safe to talk to Grandma about these things, but not your parents. Maybe it's not safe to talk with anyone in your family. People who have been abused usually respond to these family patterns of abuse either by wanting to help others—such as a younger sibling or cousin—or by forgetting about the abuse. These extremes may influence your choices and behavior as you get ready to take action.

You probably already have some idea about your family's communication style. Is it okay to talk about feelings or mistakes? Do people get angry when sensitive topics are brought up? Do family members ignore you when you talk about your feelings? These are examples of behaviors in families where it's not okay to talk about things.

What's important to remember is that it takes a lot of courage to talk about what's been happening to you. Because it's difficult, many people don't tell, and that's part of the reason abuse goes on in families for a long time, maybe even generations—because it's hard to go against the family tradition of not talking. Well, you have a choice to change that family tradition, or pattern. You can talk, and that's a great way to be strong, and begin the challenging process of change.

Desire to Protect Others

Some teens feel like they want to protect others in the family by not telling. Yet keeping quiet is really not a way to protect others or yourself. You're not responsible for taking care of others, keeping a secret, or protecting anybody from their own fears. Besides wanting to protect the abuser, you may be concerned about what will happen to younger siblings or other innocent family members if you talk about the abuse. Ask a trusted person from your support network to help you think through the possible consequences if you tell. That can help you feel less alone while you figure out how to help yourself and others.

Although you may be worried that your family will split up, whatever happens isn't your fault. Because of the abuse, relationships in your family are already more complicated than in most families. When abuse happens in families, everybody's role, or job, in the family gets mixed up. Lots of times, teens begin acting like the parents, taking care of things around the house, protecting the person who is abusing them, and feeling guilty about wanting to do things that other teens do. Sometimes distance or separation from family members is needed to help everyone figure out their own roles and identity, even if you wish they could stay together. It's not your job to keep the family together, even though you may have taken on the role of a parent or protector. If the family separates or if one of the breadwinners in your family goes to jail, it's because of the actions of the adult. By talking about what's happening, you may be able to help people in your family act like who they're supposed to be—either the parents or the kids, not some mixed-up version of a family. The whole family will be able to get help as a result of your telling.

Embarrassment

Embarrassment is another feeling that gets in the way of telling—feeling like you can't talk to anyone about this because it's too weird that it even happened to you.

You may be asking yourself, "Why is this happening to me? What's wrong with me?" Another part of what makes it hard to talk about abuse—no matter what kind it is—is that abuse isn't supposed to be happening. If it's not supposed to be happening, it can feel even more embarrassing that it's happening to you—like there's something wrong with you. That's the kind of messed-up thinking that the abuser wants you to think—it keeps you quiet. Sometimes it's hard to remember that you're not the one who did anything wrong. Abuse is the fault of the perpetrator—just because it happened to you doesn't mean it was your fault.

> If you've been raped or abused, just know that it's not your fault. I know there was nothing that I could've done.
>
> —KARLA, 16

Sometimes the topic itself is embarrassing, especially if it's sexual abuse. Many people—adults and teens—are uncomfortable talking about sex in general and might feel even more stuck with how to talk about some kind of sexual contact that isn't okay. All of these feelings about sex make it harder for you to tell. So, what's hard about talking isn't all about you—other people's feelings make it hard, too. Sometimes writing down what you want to say can help you talk about sensitive topics, or you may choose to write a letter to the person about your feelings (see page 135). It can feel easier to write things down rather than talking face-to-face, at least at first.

Relationship with the Abuser

How you feel when talking (or thinking about talking) about the abuse—to anybody—depends on what your relationship with the perpetrator was like before, during, and after the abuse. If the abuser is in your family or is a close friend, you probably have mixed feelings about telling somebody. You may feel close to this person and hate him or her at the same time. You want the abuse to stop, but you don't want the person to get in trouble. Sometimes this person feels okay in some ways and maybe even fun to be with. Some teens even talk about feeling guilty for telling. But the abuse needs to stop, and telling is the best way to make that happen, no matter how hard it might be for a while. Try to remember whose idea it was to start this behavior—not yours, right? It's important to put the responsibility where it belongs. That will help you talk to someone about what's been happening.

Remind yourself:
"The abuse needs to stop."

The relationships in your family also affect how easy or hard it might be to talk about what's happening or even to trust people. For example, if your dad was neglecting or abusing you, and Mom acts like she doesn't know or ignores you when you tell her, it becomes really hard to trust adults to take care of you. You might think that you can't be protected or that there's nothing to do to stop the abuse, but that's not true. It just feels like that inside your family. That's why you sometimes have to get help from someone outside your family, because your family may not be working very well right now. If you can, try to find someone who has experience helping teens and families with these kinds of problems. People who know how to help out teens usually have good ideas about ways to begin making changes that you may not even think about. That's why having someone else help is such a great idea. Although the solutions won't be simple and may not be easy, the more choices there are to think about, the better. For example, some teens may be so desperate to escape that they try to run away and live on their own (see Chapter 9 for more about running away). Even though running away may seem like a quick solution, it's such a hard life in reality, and can be

Mixed-up Feelings

Before you're ready to stand up for yourself, you may have to work through a lot of mixed-up feelings about what's been happening to you. Making a list of your feelings can help you understand what's happened and why you want things to change. Knowing how you feel about telling can help you understand why you've kept quiet so far and help you prepare to tell. The list below may help you understand that your feelings are normal reactions to an abnormal life event.

more unsafe than living with abuse. Asking for help from professionals can help you figure out a plan that works better for you.

Feelings About Being Abused (that might make it hard to tell)

- Enjoying some things about the abuse—gifts from the abuser, feeling special, or enjoyable physical sensations in your body

- Hating and liking the abuser at the same time

- Feeling like everybody knows what's been happening to you even though you haven't told anyone

- Feeling like you want to hide all the time—like you don't matter enough for others to care or for life to get better

- Feeling like you want to abuse someone else

- Feeling so mad that you're not sure you can control your feelings

continued ➡

- Feeling sad or crying a lot of the time
- Feeling hopeless—like things will never change
- Feeling scared that something bad will happen if you tell
- Feeling like you don't know what to do
- Feeling like it's your fault
- Feeling empty inside
- Feeling nervous and jumpy
- Feeling like nothing matters anymore
- Wishing somebody could fix this for you or rescue you, but you don't have the energy to tell
- Feeling afraid of the unknown and what will happen

Abuse as a "Normal" Part of Life

> Dad started hitting me when I was three or four. He kept doing it 'til just a couple of years ago.
> —DEVON, 14

The longer you were abused, the harder it may be to tell. You might feel more loyalty to the person who abused you, and the abuser may have made you believe it's your fault. You may think the abuse isn't so bad, because you've gotten used to it. The longer you were abused, the more mixed-up feelings you'll probably have about yourself, the abuse, and the abuser.

> I didn't even know that what Mom did was abuse until she finally let me go on a sleep-over. I realized not everybody's family was like mine. I was ten by then.
> —CASSIE, 13

If you were really young when you were first abused, you may have thought this behavior was normal for everybody, whether the abuse was sexual, physical, emotional, or neglect. Finding out it wasn't normal—like when you first stayed overnight with friends, and their families were different—was probably a big shock that you may still be getting used to. The longer the abuse lasted, the harder it may be to change because you're used to it. Sometimes, the longer it continues, the angrier you become, which can push you toward change.

Fears That Others Won't Believe You

This year my uncle said no one would believe us even if we told. He said he'd just show the pictures of Ben and me hugging, and nobody would believe there was anything wrong with that. It really felt gross.
—BEN AND BETH, 14-YEAR-OLD TWINS

Maybe it has taken you a long time to tell. It's not easy to speak up about abuse—you've been trying to understand what's happening yourself. Just because you waited to tell doesn't make the abuse any less real, and it doesn't make you responsible for it. What's important is that you're getting ready to tell. That's what counts. When you let other people know, they can help, too. Maybe then you won't feel so alone.

Sometimes teens are worried about others believing their story because the abuser is good at putting on an act for others. For example, if the abuser was somebody in your extended family, like an aunt or uncle, you might have a different relationship with that person than anybody else does in your family. Because of this difference, you might feel more hesitant to tell your family because nobody else sees your aunt or uncle as you do. You may feel like nobody will believe you and you may even begin to question your own judgment. That's dangerous. When you're feeling unsure of yourself, you're less likely to tell. Trust yourself and your memory of what happened. If you're afraid that certain people won't believe your story, turn to an adult who you know will help. (For more on deciding who to tell, see Chapter 11.)

Self-Doubt

Maybe you usually see yourself as the tough guy or tough girl, and you think you should have been able to make the abuse stop. Because you weren't able to do this, you think it's your fault. It's never your fault. You can't always control what other people do to you. Sometimes it's just not possible to make things stop without getting outside help. Asking for help is another way of being strong. Even though you may feel kind of invincible (or indestructible), sometimes things happen that make you feel less capable, or people tell you things that take away your strength, like "You're worthless" or "Nobody will believe you." That kind of feeling is one of the biggest obstacles to telling other people. But you know what? Telling is a different kind of strength. It's called empowering—taking back some of your personal power that the abuser has taken from you. Standing up for yourself can be a way of feeling better about yourself—and you don't have to do it alone.

Remind yourself:
"Telling is a different kind of strength."

Fear of What Others Will Think

People may be upset when you tell. They may be surprised or have a hard time believing this could happen. Some teens are afraid to tell their families about the abuse because they want to protect them from the emotional pain or because they're afraid of how things will change in their family. You know your own family better than anyone else. Your feelings about how they may react to news of the abuse, especially if it was committed by another family member, are probably pretty accurate. Although sometimes, adults you think you can trust may have been fooled by the abuser—so if someone responds differently than you would expect, don't give up just because they don't see what you do. They might feel angry for a while, but it's probably not at you. Sometimes what's hard is that things are going to change. It's hard for some people to change, and their anger might be more about that instead of what you've said. Some people also act mad when they're scared. Abuse can be frightening for people of any age.

You may have to figure out which will be harder for you in the long-term—accepting others' reactions or allowing the abuse to continue. Family members can get mad, and things do change, but isn't that what you wanted and needed anyway—for things to change? Doesn't the abuse have to stop for things to get better?

Wondering If You're Worth It

Abuse can make you feel worthless. You may think that nobody cares about you since no one stopped the abuse or because the abuser is treating you so badly. If emotional abuse was part of your experience, you may believe the bad things you were told about yourself. But those things *aren't* true. You're *not* a worthless person. You're a person with many positive qualities. If you have trouble thinking of good things about yourself, consider how you might be helping other people by stopping the abuse. Stopping the abuse can make sure it won't happen to anyone else. That's a great thing to feel good about.

Why Should You Tell?

Although there are many reasons not to tell, there are many more reasons to tell. The biggest reason, of course, is that telling will make it possible for the abuse to end.

Empowering

Although telling may feel frightening, it can also help you feel empowered or more in control. You're taking action to stop the abuse and take care of yourself. Even though there may be some more hard things ahead of you during the reporting and healing processes, by stopping the person from abusing you, you're winning. You're taking care of yourself and showing the abuser that you matter and that they can't control you—that's an important part of healing for you as well.

How you feel after telling depends in part on how others respond when you tell. (See Chapter 11 on deciding who to tell.) If you tell someone who supports you and takes action, you'll begin to feel protected. If you receive help and the abuse stops, you can begin to move forward in your life and feel better about yourself.

Feeling Safe

"I don't want to be around the person who did this to me any-more." That's a healthy response to abuse. When you make such a statement, what you're doing is setting boundaries. Child abuse and neglect break boundaries of trust because adults are supposed to be caring toward children. By talking about abuse or neglect—whether it's sexual, physical, or emotional—you're helping put the appropriate boundary back in place. The adults you tell can help you identify and reinforce healthy boundaries.

Preventing Others from Being Abused

Wanting to protect others from experiencing what you've been through is another common reaction, showing how much you care about other people. Telling about the abuse can make it stop for you—and for others, too. You may be worried about abuse happening to younger brothers or sisters, or cousins in your family. Some teens who are abused choose not to say anything so that the abuse continues with them and not anyone else. Maybe they've even made such a "deal" with the abuser. Although the reason behind those actions is noble, a healthier way to reach the same goal is to ask for help—it'll end up being help for yourself and others.

Remind yourself:
"I'm strong enough to speak up for myself and others."

Freedom

When you're being abused, it can feel like the abuser is in control of you. Your choices may be limited because you're preoccupied thinking about ways to avoid being hurt again. All the energy you're spending toward acting as if nothing is wrong—when some things in your life are very wrong—keeps you from having the energy to do other things that may be important to you. Abusers often like to keep you from doing things outside the family or away from their relationship, and that limits your choices as well. It's not healthy to have someone else making all those decisions for you. Part of growing up in a healthy way is learning how to make choices for yourself, hopefully with the help of a trusted adult to guide you in that process. Maybe making the decision to talk will be part of that process for you.

Feeling Better About Yourself

When someone is abusing you, it's hard to feel really good about yourself. If it's emotional abuse—the kind that happens most often, alone and with other kinds of abuse and neglect—the abuser is saying things to make you feel bad about yourself or to feel guilty. It's another kind of control. You have wonderful things to like about yourself, but you may not know what they are yet. You'll feel good about yourself when things begin to change in your life because of choices you've made. Take a chance on yourself—I bet you'll like what you discover.

A Friendlier Home

Many times, people who are abusive also drink or use other drugs, which can make their behavior even more unpredictable. It can be embarrassing to have friends over when you don't know how your parents will be acting. If they're being mean to you or the house is really messy because things aren't taken care of at home, you may not want anyone to visit you. Sometimes with sexual abuse, the abuser doesn't want you to be close to other people, so he or she may not allow you to have people over. Having friends come by to watch videos, listen to music, or just hang out is part of growing up. When the abuse stops, especially if it was happening in your family, your home may begin to change and you'll feel more comfortable inviting friends over. Even if your family doesn't change much, *you* can change, and decide what's important for you to create a healthier, happier life for yourself.

The Abuser Needs Help

Again, it's common to have mixed feelings toward the person who abused you, especially if the abuser was a family member. Part of those mixed feelings is about wanting the person to get help—so you don't have to feel confused about him or her anymore, or so the person won't abuse younger people in the family. Telling can start a process to help the abuser learn other ways of connecting with people, feeling good about himself or herself, learning how to express love and take care of loved ones, or expressing frustrations in a more healthy manner. This may take the abuser a long time, but it will be better for everybody after that hard work is done.

> I want him to go to jail. If he doesn't, he probably won't be cured. Dad has a girlfriend with a four-year-old son. I worry that he will abuse him.
>
> —MARTA, 14

***

Deciding to tell others is a big deal—and it's not easy. But it's a step you must take in order to begin feeling safe. Every day you go without telling is another day the abuser is controlling you. Take back your life.

Let It Out

Remember, writing in a journal is a great way to help you figure exactly what's going on in your life and how you feel about it. It's private and usually feels like a safer place to start than talking to someone face-to-face. It's okay if you don't feel ready to do any journaling. Respect yourself and your own pace. Just do those things that you feel ready to do.

- What are your fears about telling others about the abuse?
- What good things will happen after you tell?

CHAPTER 11

Telling Others

Maybe you've decided that you're ready to try talking with someone. That's a great decision.

Who Should You Tell?

Once you decide to talk, you have to decide who to talk to: someone inside your family or outside your family? You can even make a hotline call yourself if you can't figure out a safe person you know to tell (see pages 83–84 in Chapter 9). There are lots of people—at your school, at social service agencies, at places of worship—who want to help if you've been abused and most of them are required or "mandated" by law to help. It's often convenient to talk to someone at school—like a counselor, teacher, coach, or club sponsor. Maybe you have a close friend whose parents could help. What's important is to pick someone who you think will believe you and will be able to help with what you need right now. Maybe you just need someone to listen and feel like he or she is on your side.

Mandatory Reporters

"Mandatory reporters" is a legal term for professionals who are required (by law) to call the child abuse hotline to report abuse that they've learned about or suspect is going on. Mandatory reporters are people who are part of your everyday life—teachers, counselors, doctors, nurses, other health care providers, and police, like DARE officers at your school. Any of these people are good resources to whom you can safely report abuse. They're required to contact authorities to help stop the abuse.

Ask yourself these questions about the person you're thinking about telling:

- Does this person usually support me unconditionally?

- Do I feel like this person will help me out even if I say something he or she finds surprising or hard to believe?

- What kind of relationship does this person have with the abuser?
- Will this person's relationship with the abuser make it harder or easier for me to be completely honest about what happened?

You may want to talk about your answers to these questions with a trusted adult or review your feelings in your journal pages.

Ms. Cotter had been my teacher in grade school—now she was the counselor at my school. I guess she could tell I wasn't feeling so good or something because she came up and started talking to me. I just spilled out everything about what happened. It felt good to finally tell someone.

—Nikki, 16

How Do You Tell?

There isn't an exact formula on how to tell someone you've been abused. It's different for everybody. In general, however, it's usually best to be simple and direct when choosing your words to tell. Here are some examples:

- "I need your help."
- "I have a problem that I feel really scared about."
- "I don't know what to do. My dad's abusing me."
- "Things at home aren't so good. Can you help me?"
- "I have a big change to make and don't know how to do it."
- "This is really hard for me to say, but somebody's been abusing me. I don't know how to make it stop."
- "I'm feeling sad about something."
- "I'm feeling stuck."
- "I need some ideas."

Use these ideas as a starting point. It often feels easier to open the conversation by talking about things generally. Then, when you see that the other person is interested and wants to help, you can just keep talking—explaining what the big problem is. Your readiness to talk will help the words come once you get started. Having someone listen as you talk about secrets you've been keeping inside a long time can feel good enough to make you forget your fears or embarrassment, at least for a while. Many people who tell feel really good for a while—maybe hours, maybe days. But then, the old feelings of questioning oneself may creep back in— feeling scared, ashamed, even wondering about the decision to tell. Bouncing back and forth between feeling good and not so good can be a normal part of telling. Over time, you will have less and less bad feelings, and more and more positive feelings about all that you have done. Having people around who believe you and support you helps you feel less alone, and better about yourself.

Remind yourself:
"It will feel good to have someone really listen to me."

My summer was watching TV with my stepdad. He was home on disability. I told Mom I didn't like hanging out with him, but she didn't get it. She just went on and on about how hard it is for her to keep the family together. She actually asked me to be a trooper and help the family out for once. It felt like I told her and she didn't listen.

—SARAH, 13

It may feel hard to be direct about telling. Maybe you think people around you should know something's wrong, but they might not. They may not pick up on your clues or hints that something's wrong. That's why being direct is necessary. No matter how close you are to people around you, they cannot know what's going on in your mind—if you don't tell them why you don't want to go with Uncle Ted, they may assume you're just being "difficult" or "selfish" and make you go anyway. You need to tell them what's really going on to get them to help and to put a stop to it for good.

Sometimes People Find Out Even If You Don't Tell

Sometimes your behavior may start telling about the abuse for you—this is okay, too. Just be honest when adults ask if something has happened. It doesn't matter how you tell, as long as you talk with someone about the abuse. That's part of the hard work that you have to do to make things better. It might feel unfair that you have to work so hard to get through something that wasn't your fault, but it's worth it. Here are some ways your behavior may alert others that something is wrong:

Clues That Something's Bothering You

- Mood changes, crying spells
- Feeling mad or irritable a lot
- Not feeling anything—feeling numb
- Wanting to get really close to others or be really distant from them
- Doing lots of drinking or drugs
- Wanting to or having sex
- Having more headaches or stomachaches than usual
- Not sleeping well
- Eating more or less
- Not taking care of yourself
- Hurting yourself, like cutting, scratching, or burning
- Not caring about yourself or what happens to you
- Feeling like there's nothing to look forward to
- Changes in grades at school
- Trouble concentrating during class—like daydreams or negative thoughts

Remind yourself:
"Working through the abuse will be worth it."

Making a Plan

You've decided or have at least thought about who to tell about the abuse. That's a positive and very important step. Creating a detailed plan on how to tell is another step you can take as you get ready to tell. You can write out your plan in your journal, on a piece of paper you can carry with you, or you can just think about it, if that's more comfortable for you. Your plan should include the following parts:

The person I'll tell first:

This is when I'll tell this person:

This is where I'll tell this person:

Here's what I'll say:

I think the person will respond in this way:

If I don't get a positive, helpful response, I'll tell this person next:

Tori's Plan to Talk About the Abuse

The person I'll tell first: My school counselor, Ms. Jennings.

This is when I'll tell this person: I'm going in to tell her Monday morning.

This is where I'll tell this person: I will drop by her office before my first class.

Here's what I'll say: Ms. Jennings, I have a problem. I need your help. (I know I'm going to cry, so I'll close her door before I start talking.)

I think the person will respond in this way: Ms. Jennings will probably be surprised, but I think she'll know what to do.

continued ➡

If I don't get a positive, helpful response, I'll tell this person next:
Ms. Jennings is a safe person to tell because she has to help me, but I know she would anyway. If she doesn't help me or says she's too busy before I get a chance to say anything, I'm going to talk to my music teacher, Mr. Backer. If he doesn't help either, I might call the hotline myself, but I'll ask my friend Katie to do it with me. I feel scared, but I have to do this—I'm ready.

What Should You Expect When You Tell?

You may feel more confident telling others about the abuse if you've thought about how they might react. An individual's reaction to hearing that you've been abused can range from loving support to disbelief and everything in between, depending on a number of factors. It's impossible to know how a person will react, but being prepared and playing through different situations in your mind can help you feel stronger when you talk.

Here are some reactions other teens have received when they told about being abused:

- "Mom acted like she didn't even hear me. I think she was scared."

- "My aunt told me I could live with her. She offered to come right over and get me. I said okay."

- "My dad got mad and blamed me—he always thinks sex is the girl's fault."

- "My dad blamed me—he called me a 'fag' and threatened to kick me out of the house."

- "My mom called the police immediately. Then she called a counselor and got me an appointment to talk about my feelings. She confronted my dad when he got home and told him he had to stay the night somewhere else or we were going to. Dad left."

- "My mom looked sad and surprised and scared, but she listened to what happened. Then she hugged me and said it would be okay."

- ■ "My school counselor called the hotline while I was in her office. She told me it might be hard, but I had done the right thing. That felt good."
- ■ "I called the hotline. They said they'd send someone right over. The police were at my house in a few minutes."

You need to be prepared that adults in your family may not fully support you in your attempts to stop the abuse or talk about it. You might not feel like they believe you, or you might think that they've known what was happening but didn't try to protect you. This may be because of the relationship they have with the abuser. Also, if the person in your family you want to tell is also being abused or scared by this person, they may not be able to help you very well. They may want you to stay quiet, too—not to be mean, but because of their own fears. If you feel unprotected in your family after you tell, find someone outside your family to help you.

Getting mixed reactions from people outside your family can also happen (even though it shouldn't). If you choose to tell a coach, a teacher, or even some counselors, you may not get the kind of support that you expect. It can feel really bad when someone who's supposed to help doesn't. Don't let those reactions stop you. Keep in mind what you need for yourself, and remember that there are people who want to help you. Even though it doesn't feel right that you have to tell again and again, you may have to do that to find someone who you can trust and who is willing to help you. Everybody has their own definitions of abuse and neglect, mostly based on their own experiences. If somebody thinks what you've experienced isn't "bad enough" for them to help, go find someone else to talk to. You will find someone who can be there for you.

Talking about what happened to me was really hard. I was afraid my friend would think I was gross because my father abused me. Crystal was really great. She went with me to my school counselor, and I started talking. A lot of things have changed since I first started talking, but I'm not getting hurt anymore. That feels great.

—CAMIE, 15

How Do You Cope with Feelings?

As you prepare to tell others about the abuse, you probably feel nervous. It can be helpful at this time to think about how you cope with stress. Here are some common ways of coping and helping yourself feel strong enough to tell about what's happening—to ask for help.

Ways to Cope as You Get Ready to Talk

- Talk to a friend.
- Ask a trusted adult about how they might help somebody with a problem.
- Write down what you want to say.
- Practice what you are going to say—like a speech.
- Have a back-up plan—what happens if they don't believe me?
- Ask someone to help you talk about it—maybe even be there with you.
- Imagine yourself being successful talking about the abuse.
- Take deep breaths when you feel nervous or scared.
- Think about how good you will feel when it stops.
- Use physical exercise to help you cope with feeling nervous or stressed.
- See yourself as a hero for taking care of yourself.

What Happens If You Don't Tell?

It is your choice to tell or not, but like any choice, this one has consequences. If you choose not to tell, the abuse will probably continue—if not against you, against someone else. Even if the abuse stops without your telling, you'll probably need to talk about it at some point or those feelings and memories will stay inside you. Although the feelings and thoughts may seem to be forgotten, it's more like they get buried and come back up later. When thoughts or feelings about the abuse come back, they can come in the form of nightmares or flashbacks. (See pages 166–167 for more about flashbacks.) These thoughts or feelings may not seem related to anything that's going on in your life right now. The feelings can be subtle or strong—ranging from nervousness or worry to being immobilized by terror. Behaviors may also be less direct expressions of abuse, ranging from mad acting out, sexual acting out, using drugs or drinking, feeling all alone or like you want to hide, to trouble being close to others.

Talking about abuse is difficult and you don't have to do it, but it's important to know that it's also hard if you don't talk about it. At least if you begin to talk about the abuse, then you're starting a process of making things better.

Remind yourself:
"Feeling better is what it's all about."

What If You Aren't Ready to Tell?

If you aren't ready to tell, you need to respect those feelings. However, you also need to think about whether those feelings are your own or have been influenced by the abuser. The abuser doesn't want you to talk about what's happening and may have influenced you in many different ways. It's possible that you're confusing what the abuser wants you to feel with your own feelings.

Try journaling about what you think would happen if you choose to talk about the abuse. What feelings do you have? What are you afraid will happen? Are you able to see anything good come out of talking about the abuse or neglect?

If after exploring your feelings about the abuse you choose not to tell, try to think of ways to make yourself safer. Are there activities you can get involved in at school or church that will keep you too busy to be around the abuser? What other plans can you develop to keep yourself safe? Make a list.

***

Sometimes getting someone to listen feels hard—you may have to keep trying until you find someone who can help. Keep going; keep talking until someone helps. You're worth the effort.

Let It Out

Remember, writing in a journal is a great way to help you figure exactly what's going on in your life and how you feel about it. It's private and usually feels like a safer place to start than talking to someone face-to-face. It's okay if you don't feel ready to do any journaling. Respect yourself and your own pace. Just do those things that you feel ready to do.

■ Make a list of safe people with whom you could share your feelings and experiences about the abuse.

■ Write out your script for talking to:

a parent

a counselor

a teacher

a friend

CHAPTER 12

What Happens After I Tell?

You've done it! You've broken the silence and told someone else about the abuse. That took a lot of strength and courage. It wasn't easy, but you came forward, told what happened, and asked for help. Good for you.

Who Are All These People and Why Are They in Your Life Now?

You're probably wondering what's next. What will happen now that someone else knows what you've been going through? If you've told a trusting adult who will take action, things will get better. Depending on the type of abuse you've suffered and the severity of it, a number of different authorities may become involved in your life for a while to help you. This will happen for all kinds of abuse as well as neglect. You're not alone dealing with the abuse anymore.

Here are some of the people who may enter your life:

Teachers. You may have turned to a teacher when you decided to talk about the abuse. Teachers can continue to provide support as you talk with Child Protective Services and other professionals working on your case. Teachers may also be helpful in managing your school workload. If they know you're going through a challenging time, most teachers will be willing to adjust your assignments or due dates—which can make a big difference in your stress level. Don't be afraid to ask for the help you need.

Therapists/counselors. Therapists or counselors can provide support throughout all phases of the process following your telling about the abuse. In addition, some therapists, psychologists, or counselors may meet with you at the request of Child Protective

Services or the Division of Family Services to evaluate your situation. These evaluations are usually limited to just a few sessions and focus on what's happened to you and how you feel about it. This information is usually shared with family services and, in some cases, the police, attorneys, and a judge. Parents usually do not see these evaluations, or reports; however a parent's attorney may allow a parent to view the report during a trial.

Social Workers/DFS Workers. Social workers or people from your county's Division of Family or Social Services (DFS or DSS) usually become involved very early in the "investigation." They'll interview you as soon as possible so they can begin to determine how to keep you safe.

Doctors. When doctors become involved with cases of abuse or neglect, they have an "investigative" role. For physical or sexual abuse, doctors will often examine you and take photographs, documenting the abuse (for example, bruises, cuts, or scratches).

Law Enforcement. Law enforcement, or police officers, may become part of the investigation at different points, depending on who the abuse was reported to. If it was reported directly to them, they'll become involved right away. If Family Services or Child Protective Services received the initial report of abuse, and has been able to manage the situation to ensure your safety, the police may not become involved until after the initial investigation has been completed and the information is shared with them. The exact procedure or order in which professionals become involved may differ slightly from state to state.

Attorneys. Lawyers, or attorneys, act as advocates for people in the legal or court system. In cases of abuse or neglect, the job of the lawyers who work on your case is to convince the judge that your experience meets the standard of abuse defined by the law. You'll probably be working with the prosecuting attorney or an attorney from the family court system.

Judges. The judge, and sometimes a jury, listens to all the evidence or information in a case and then decides whether the person who abused you can be called "guilty" according to the law.

Many child abuse cases are decided by a judge to keep your identity protected from the public.

Court. In a formal way, court refers to the judge and his or her decision. Court also can refer to the physical space where a trial occurs. For juvenile hearings—including cases involving child abuse—the courtroom is often closed to the public. This means there won't be lots of people walking in and out of the courtroom and your privacy as a minor will be protected.

Here are some terms that you may hear during the legal part of your case:

■ *Investigation:* The process of authorities and professionals meeting with you and talking about what happened. An investigation usually involves separate meetings with you and your parents, and may involve other family members, friends, or baby-sitters. An investigation may stop with the family services agency recommending changes in your family, or it may continue to a legal phase. Again, how far into the legal system your "case" goes depends on the severity of the abuse and on the laws where you live.

■ *Allegations:* Police or DFS workers might use the term "alleged abuse" or "suspected abuse" for legal reasons. The language they use doesn't mean they don't believe you. Until an investigation is complete—which includes talking with you and sometimes going to court—the authorities cannot legally call what's happened to you "abuse" or "neglect." You can call it that, and your counselor or therapist may also give it that label, but other authorities probably won't use those terms until after the legal proceedings. Don't let their use of other words—for example, "alleged abuse"—make you doubt yourself or your story.

■ *Case:* this word is used by authorities to describe all the aspects involved in the investigation of your abuse. The "case" may include information from you, interviews with the person who abused you, and anything decided in court.

■ *Substantiated:* Family Services or Child Protective Services and the police use this term when the information gathered during their investigation meets the standards that says abuse or neglect occurred.

- *Unsubstantiated:* Family Services or Child Protective Services use this term when the information gathered during their investigation doesn't meet the standards that say abuse or neglect occurred.

- *Severity:* This term used by professionals and authorities actually has several parts, including:

  - frequency (how often incidents of abuse occur)

  - duration (how long it's been happening to you)

  - use of force or violence

  - type of abuse (physical, emotional, sexual, neglect, or a combination of any of these

  - specific acts committed during the abuse (these include the examples listed in Chapters 2–5)

What Exactly Will Happen Next?

Telling Your Story Again

After you've told a mandatory reporter, authorities will begin investigating the reported abuse or allegations. The "authorities" might include someone from the police or sheriff's department or DFS.

They'll usually start by interviewing you, which means you'll have to tell your story to more adults. Professionals in most communities do try to coordinate interviews so you won't have to retell your story too many times, but you'll probably have to repeat it at least one more time after the first time you tell. No matter how many people you end up talking with during the investigation and, perhaps, court proceedings, just try to tell the truth. Don't let attorneys or other adults confuse you or make you doubt your own statements. If you begin to feel pressured or confused, ask for a break. It's okay to take care of yourself.

The professionals who will be interviewing you are used to working with teens who have been abused, and they know what kinds of bad things happen in abuse. Your stories won't surprise them.

Interviews by these authorities can take place at your school or at your home. Your parents may not know about the interview, at first. Parents don't have to give permission for these authorities to talk to you about the reported abuse. The authorities will also talk to your parents, usually at your home.

When the DFS workers or police meet with you, they'll ask you to explain, in your own words, what's been happening to you. After listening to you, they'll be able to decide what should happen next to get you safe. They will act as quickly as possible. If the abuse is recent or ongoing, you will probably not be able to go back and be with the abuser without a social worker or police officer going with you. It's important to remember that these professionals have your best interests in mind. They're going to work to protect you and advocate for you.

Feelings About Talking to Authorities

Although having other people know about the "secret" may be frightening or uncomfortable, it can help you. These people, and the state laws that help them protect you, are there to stop the abuse and help you get safe. You've taken the first step on your own, and now others are there to help you continue.

When you talk to authorities, you may feel scared at first. Part of being scared comes from feeling out of control. This is normal. Some things about feeling out of control may even be familiar to you from your experience of abuse. Realistically, you probably had less control before telling about the abuse than you have now. What's important to remember is that you're taking action that will help you gain control over part of your life. But at first you might feel mixed up and uncomfortable around these strangers who are talking with you about such personal things, especially if your parents don't know. You might feel embarrassed because you weren't able to protect yourself or even that the abuse happened to you at all. You might feel confused if the abuser was someone you thought you could trust and this person hurt you or made you feel bad about yourself. It might feel like you're breaking a promise by talking, but you need to talk about what happened. Anything you might have said or done with the abuser was an attempt to survive—that's what anyone does when feeling threatened. You may be breaking a promise, but you are not bound to keep a promise made under abusive threats. That kind of promise is different than other kinds of promises you might make. By telling, you're being brave and taking care of yourself.

Sometimes it can feel uncomfortable just because you're doing something differently than you have in the past—talking is doing something differently— telling the secret or changing a familiar

Your Support Network

Now might be a good time to review the list of people in your support network (see pages 84–85), as you may begin to recognize needs you didn't have before. For example, you might need "cheerleaders" to support and encourage you. You might need "experts" to explain more about the investigation or the legal process. You might need professionals, such as counselors or psychologists, to help you learn ways to adapt to these changes in your life and cope with stress from change.

behavior or habit. You might also be worried that the abuser will hurt you, say that you're lying, or hurt someone else in your family. All these mixed-up feelings make it hard to keep talking. That's why it's so important for you to be able to trust the people outside your family who are trying to help you, as well as to trust in yourself about the knowledge that you were abused. (You may want to review the basic definitions in Chapter 1—to give you words to talk about what happened and to give yourself permission to call the things that happened to you "abuse.")

Although it can be frightening to talk to so many different people about such personal things, talking can help you work through your feelings about the abuse—and this is healthy.

Remind yourself:
"I have lots of people to help me."

What If You Change Your Mind?

Sometimes people who have been abused take back, or recant, their story after the investigation begins. Often, this happens because the person is scared or worried about what lies ahead.

I'm afraid things will go wrong in court.

—Drew, 14

It may be hard to stick with your story if you get scared or confused, but taking back your story won't make things go back to the more familiar way things were. The investigation will continue because the people you told believe you and because the perpetrator may also be doing the same things to other people. The authorities will want to protect other potential victims as well as you. Also, if you take back your story, you won't have protection from the abuser and, unfortunately, the abuser may treat you even worse for telling. This is hard to remember when you're feeling confused and upset about all the changes going on since you told, but it's important to keep yourself from greater danger by sticking with your story. With the help of safe people, the problems you're experiencing with all the changes will get better in time.

Going to Court

Child abuse and neglect are not only wrong—they're also against the law. In cases of substantiated abuse or neglect, legal action may be called for to keep you safe and to make changes for the abuser and your family.

Cases may lead to a trial if the abuser denies the charges of abuse or neglect. When this happens, someone must bring charges against the perpetrator. For some people who have been abused, going to court feels empowering because they're taking action against the abuser. For others, going to court feels too scary, so they may not want to press charges. Although your wishes will be heard, advocates and workers in the system may decide to proceed anyway even if you'd rather not. In most states, authorities have the right to bring charges, with or without the support of the person who was abused. The role of the authorities is to protect people, and you're included in that effort. They may decide to take action, even if you're not feeling ready, because they want to protect you. If you recognize that letting them do their job will help you feel better over time, you may feel less nervous about what's happening. If the case goes to court against your wishes, you may feel more anxious and nervous about it than if you and your family decided to proceed.

Until you're 18, you won't be able to press charges yourself. Those advocating for you and working with you will have to do so. Your parents can also file charges on your behalf. If no one presses charges, or you live in a state where the authorities don't have the right to bring charges themselves, the case of your abuse or neglect may not go to court, however if "substantiated," the legal system usually becomes involved.

Child abuse cases are heard and decided by a judge in most cases. A jury may be involved, depending on what kind of legal charges are being brought against the perpetrator. During the trial, the attorneys representing you and your case will present evidence about what happened to you. You and other witnesses may also be questioned. After both sides present their version of what happened, the judge will make a decision. If your abuser is found "not guilty," it doesn't mean the judge thought you were lying—it just means the evidence in the case didn't meet the standards of the law that defines abuse.

Taking Care of Yourself

Although you're not the one on trial, going to court can still be stressful. You're probably dealing with a lot of feelings and memories. Using visual imagery can relieve stress by helping you see yourself as able to cope with stressors. This coping strategy is kind of like what athletes use to enhance their performance for a race or game. Here's how: Imagine yourself in the courtroom. If you see the perpetrator, imagine him or her as helpless. Even if the abuser tries to speak, no words come out of his or her mouth. As you tell your story, imagine yourself feeling empowered and in control of the situation. Remember that powerful feeling during the court case. Other things that can help are relaxation strategies, such as deep breathing, meditation, or listening to relaxing music.

There are also other strategies to use in the courtroom. For example, don't look at the abuser while he or she is talking or while you're talking. Look at your attorney, a supportive person from Child Protective Services, the police, or your family. Try to "tune out" or not listen to what the abuser is saying. If you feel really nervous, tell your attorney that you need a "recess" or a break from the proceedings. They will want to help

continued ➡

you feel as comfortable as possible during the court proceedings. Because attorneys work in the courtroom almost every day, they may have more suggestions for you. Listen to them—they're an advocate for you.

Results from investigations or court proceedings can vary greatly. If the abuse was very severe and was committed by a parent, the court may decide that your parents cannot learn to take care of you, even with help from agencies. In such situations, the judge may "terminate" their "parental rights." This means that they would no longer be legally responsible, or able to act as your parents. Biologically, of course, they'd still be your parents, but you wouldn't be seeing them on a regular basis (if at all), and they wouldn't be involved in any of the decisions about raising you or have the financial obligations that parents have. The process of terminating parental rights takes a long time; it could be a few years before such an action is finalized. Your day-to-day life will have changed long before that final court action. Part of that change might include being placed in foster care or with a relative who serves as a foster parent (see pages 123–124 for more on foster care).

Here are some other potential outcomes when severe abuse occurs within the family:

■ The perpetrator may be asked to move out of the home.

■ The abuser and/or your family may be required to participate in counseling.

■ The abuser may serve some time in jail or on probation.

Feelings About Going to Court

Feelings of anxiety are normal around court proceedings for many reasons:

■ The abuser will be in the courtroom.

■ There are a lot of things that may feel out of your control about the proceedings, no matter how much the system tries to protect you.

■ It may feel like you're being blamed for the abuse by the abuser's attorney.

■ It's difficult to talk about the abuse in front of people you don't know and in front of the abuser.

Professionals who work with the court and with people who have been abused know how difficult the process can be. They'll try to help you by giving you as much information as they can and preparing you for the trial. They can serve as advocates for you in the legal process. Being an advocate means they can sometimes act for you while in court or during the process.

Taking a Break

Dealing with abuse is hard, and it doesn't get easier immediately after you tell. It's just really tough stuff and there's no way around it. Even though you're going to feel challenged as you're going through this time, it's important to take care of yourself. The ideas below can help you take care of yourself as you're working through the issues associated with your abusive experiences. Try doing things on this list or come up with some of your own ways to give yourself a break during this stressful time:

■ Go to a funny movie with a friend.

■ Write in your journal.

■ Lose yourself in a good book.

■ Exercise.

■ Have a video game contest with a group of friends.

Sometimes the prosecuting attorney may help set up special meetings with the judge or other attorneys to take your statements outside of court. These meetings outside of court are called depositions, a legal term for sitting down with attorneys and a court reporter to record your answers to certain questions and put it on paper for the judge to read. A person called a "guardian ad litem"— an attorney, mental health professional, volunteer, or another community member appointed by a judge—will probably be appointed to act on your behalf and advocate for your best interests.

Court systems want to try to make it as easy for you as possible, while still giving the accused person his or her full legal rights. This part of the legal system is often hard to take. You may feel legitimately angry because of all the hard things you have to go through because of what someone else did. That's why advocates are there, because they know how to make the process easier, so ask for what you need. For example, if you want to know more about what will happen, ask to visit the courtroom to see what it looks like and how it feels to sit in the witness chair. They may help you role-play the courtroom scene.

During the trial, remember that you don't have to look at your abuser—it's probably best not to. Look at the prosecuting attorney, your guardian ad litem, or the judge. You should have a friend or trusted adult come for support. Maybe the person who you first disclosed the abuse to would be a good support person.

Here are some terms that you may hear if your case goes to court:

■ *Prosecuting attorney:* an attorney working for the state or government whose job is to prove that the accused person's behavior violated the law.

■ *Defense attorney:* an attorney working on behalf of the person accused of abusing you.

■ *Testify:* This is speaking under oath in court. Speaking under oath means that you promise to "tell the truth" about everything you're asked. Telling a lie when you testify is against the law and is called perjury.

For some teens who have felt angry for a while, the trial may be therapeutic and empowering. It might make you feel stronger and help you reclaim positive feelings about yourself. The trial can be a big part of healing.

Remind yourself:
"Telling was something I did for me."

When my family's lawyer told me I'd have to go to court about my cousin, I thought I could handle it. Part of me even thought it would feel good, but as it got closer, I thought I was going to totally freak out. I started having nightmares and felt

continued ➡

like he was watching me wherever I went. I was almost afraid to get off the bus after school 'cause I knew nobody else would be home for a while.

My counselor helped me understand what it would be like in court and said I should ask my lawyer to take me to the courtroom before the trial. This helped a lot. I'm so glad I did that. They told me about not having to look at him even though he was in the same room. The trial day was the first time I'd seen him since I had talked about what he did. I was so scared. My hands were all sweaty and my voice was shaky, but I did it. I just looked at my lawyer. His lawyer was tricky and stood right next to him, trying to get me all scared by looking at him, but I did what my lawyer said and looked at my lawyer or the judge. It felt a whole lot safer, like my cousin wasn't even there.

Even though it was hard, I felt a whole lot stronger and better after it was over. My cousin did get jail time—not enough I thought, for what he did to me, but it felt good to know that I was taking control of some stuff now that I could. Everybody that mattered said they felt proud of me, even though I was kind of embarrassed about what they'd think.

—HANNAH, 16

Seeing a Doctor

Another part of the investigation may include an exam for physical evidence. For physical abuse, it involves a thorough and complete physical exam, including taking pictures of any bruising and possibly X-rays for new and old broken bones. Another exam is completed if sexual abuse is suspected. It is called the SAFE exam, or Sexual Abuse Forensic Examination. The purpose of the exam is to find out—by a doctor or nurse physically examining and sometimes taking pictures of your genitals and anus—whether physical evidence of sexual abuse exists. Some people think such exams are embarrassing, especially if you haven't had such an exam before. The exam may also make you think about the abuse again or remember times you were abused, depending on what kinds of things happened to you. Try to trust the doctors and nurses, but don't hesitate to speak up if *anything* makes you uncomfortable. They know how hard the exams can be, and they'll try to make it as easy for you as possible. If you think it would be helpful, you can ask someone you trust, for example, your guardian or counselor, to be with you for the exam.

Getting Counseling

Counseling can be a really important part of your healing process. Therapists and counselors can help you:

- work through your feelings about telling
- grieve for what you've experienced and what you've lost
- accept that relationships with the abuser and others have changed—learning what that means for you
- develop strategies to deal with symptoms related to the abuse—like feeling down, feeling nervous, crying, being angry, having flashbacks, memories, or nightmares
- express feelings in a healthy way
- learn to cope with changes and challenges in your life
- adjust to being in foster care
- role-play what you might say in court or to others in talking about the abuse
- identify what you want for yourself and what kind of person you want to be now that the abuse has stopped

Remind yourself:
"I know how to ask for help when something new comes up."

Child Protective Services often helps arrange counseling, or you can ask for help in finding someone to work with. Talk with your case manager from Child Protective Services about how your work is going with your counselor or therapist. If you don't feel comfortable, the counseling won't be as effective. Speaking up is a way of taking care of yourself. That's an important part of counseling as well—learning to talk about your feelings and work through uncomfortable and hard issues about what's happened to you.

> My aunt's husband abused me since I was 9 or 10, and I didn't tell anybody until now. I think I just tried to forget about it. After I told, it stopped, but I was really scared I would see him around town, and he would know I told. I told the police. I talked to a therapist. My lawyer told me to. I was scared about going to court, too. I really wanted him to get punished, but I was still scared of him. I felt like I was still being kind of abused.
>
> —REBECCA, 14

Foster Care

Each state has its own foster care system to take care of children who cannot live with their parents for a time—for whatever reason. Often, kids who are abused are temporarily placed in foster care after the abuse has been reported. Being in foster care usually means that you live with a different family, or sometimes another member of your own family. About 20 percent of all cases of child abuse and neglect—ranging from 2 percent placement in some states to 60 percent in others—result in a foster care placement.[1]

Some teens think the idea of foster care sounds a little frightening. Part of that fear often comes just from not knowing what will happen. Being placed in foster care might mean staying overnight with a foster family as Child Protective Services is developing a plan for your safety. Staying with a foster family may also last longer.

Depending on how old you are at the time of placement, and the treatment plans for your family, your length of time in foster care will vary. At some point, you may return to live with your non-abusive parent and possibly the abusing parent. This depends on a number of things, including how well your parents follow through with treatment recommendations made by Child Protective Services. If time in jail is ordered for your abusing parent, he or she might be returned to your home after incarceration. The authorities have a responsibility to help the abuser make changes for themselves and changes in how they interact with other people—including you. If anything feels uncomfortable to you—like being around the abuser, tell your counselor or Child Protective Services. They can help make sure that the abuser is working on making big changes, too. Sometimes teens who are placed in foster care can be adopted, depending on their age and the identity of their abusers. If both parents were abusive, and you were young at the time of placement, adoption could be an option.

Other factors affecting the length of your placement include how your non-abusive parent is able to support you—emotionally and financially. Sometimes the parent who didn't abuse continues to have difficulty accepting that the other parent could do so. If those feelings are very strong, it'll be difficult for you to remain in your home. This situation may make you feel abandoned by your parents. You may also feel angry about being placed in foster care. All these feelings are normal, but foster care is one way to ensure your safety, and that's what Child Protective Services are interested in doing. Most foster families are caring and kind. If you find that you don't feel safe with yours, it's important to let your social worker or case manager know. You might remember that the social worker or case manager is the person who works with Child Protective Services, and coordinates things that are happening to you in this process of talking about abuse.

***

Who knew that telling about the abuse would expose you to so many new and different people? Many teens who have been abused and exposed to the system find the experience so helpful that they eventually choose to work in fields of social work, law enforcement, or law to help protect others. Giving back to others by helping them is a good way to help yourself. Make something positive out of a traumatic time in your life. It's a wonderful feeling to be able to "bounce back," to be resilient. Sometimes hard things push us to become who we really are. I hope that you are learning all about your strengths and are feeling better and better about who you are.

Let It Out

Remember, writing in a journal is a great way to help you figure exactly what's going on in your life and how you feel about it. It's private and usually feels like a safer place to start than talking to someone face-to-face. It's okay if you don't feel ready to do any journaling. Respect yourself and your own pace. Just do those things that you feel ready to do.

- What do you need to help you feel stronger about testifying? For example, look at others in the courtroom like your attorney or friends who are there.

- Since you've told others about the abuse, some things in your life may be changing. What are those changes and how are feeling about them?

CHAPTER 13

Helping a Friend Who Has Been Abused

Sometimes, you may suspect something's going on with one of your friends, notice that the person is struggling with a decision, or is feeling bad. Even though you may be good friends, it can be hard for people—even close friends—to talk about being abused.

You might notice changes in the way your friend acts. Perhaps he or she has suddenly started having sex, is being mean or aggressive, or has just quit hanging out with other people. When things are really hard to talk about, bodies and behaviors have a way of expressing what's really going on. This sometimes happens when people have been abused. (See page 103 in Chapter 11 to learn more about behavioral clues.)

> My friend Krissy started acting weird—like she was all afraid or something. She didn't want to hang out downtown anymore or come over at night. It went on for a couple of weeks, and she just ignored my questions. Finally, I told her she was acting like something bad happened to her, and she started crying. I sat with her when she told her mom about her cousin raping her.
>
> —Tamara, 16

How Can You Be Supportive?

What should you do if you think your friend has been abused? It's probably not best to directly ask your friend if that's what is going on. Your friend is likely to deny it. This denial doesn't mean he or she doesn't trust you—people who have been abused are simply used to denying abuse. It's how they cope with it. Here are some ways that you can help your friend:

■ Tell your friend you're worried about him or her. If the person brushes off your concern, ask if he or she will read a book that might be helpful. Then offer your friend this book or other helpful resources you've found.

■ Tell your friend that you're concerned about how he or she feels and you want to help. Invite your friend for an overnight so you can talk, or suggest talking together with your school counselor.

■ If you've had any experiences of abuse or know someone who has, share this with your friend. This will help your friend see how often abuse actually happens—he or she isn't alone.

■ Help your friend see that his or her reactions to the abuse are normal—what's happened to him or her isn't.

■ Encourage your friend to express his or her feelings by talking, writing, or drawing a picture—or in any other way that feels comfortable.

■ Let your friend know you're there for him or her.

■ If your friend is in physical danger and refuses your help, talk to a trusted adult yourself, or call a local abuse hotline or the national hotline at 1-800-422-4453.

Remind yourself:
"I care enough about my friend to help
(or ask for help)."

When a friend is going through a rough time, it's not always easy to be patient and supportive. Sometimes you may be tempted to ignore your friend's behavioral clues, especially if the person continues to deny that anything's wrong—but you can clearly see that something's changed and he or she is behaving differently than in the past. You may also feel angry if you think your friend isn't being honest with you. Why is your friend lying to you? It's important to remember that your friend may be "lying" to everyone about being abused—including himself or herself. Lying to oneself in this way is a psychological defense mechanism—it's a way to fool yourself into thinking that something bad hasn't happened. Things that will not be helpful to your friend include:

- ignoring changes in your friend

- staying angry or irritated with your friend

- keeping your concerns to yourself

- letting your friend drift away from you, other friends, and activities

- watching your friend make choices that are unhealthy, and doing nothing

> My friend Tom just kind of checked out from life when he was about 13. Looking back, I wish I had talked to him then. It wasn't until the creep who abused him got arrested that any of us knew for sure what had happened to Tom. I felt like I'd let a friend down 'cause I didn't do anything. I knew he was acting weird, but I would never have guessed why. Now I know that guys can get abused, too.
> —DAVID, 17

What If My Friend Is Depressed or Suicidal?

Many people who feel defeated and unable to make changes in their lives—common feelings for people who have been abused—become depressed. Depression can sometimes feel so bad that people can't come up with a solution or a way out, and so they think about suicide. Here are some signs of depression and suicide:

Warning Signs of Depression and Suicide

- sadness or crying

- overwhelming feelings of pain

- hopelessness

- wanting to be alone

- feeling worthless

- getting mad easily

- being mean to friends

- not taking care of oneself—like not showering or changing clothes

- hurting oneself

- changes in daily life, like sleeping or eating habits, or not doing homework

- no longer enjoying fun or school activities like before

- talking about plans to kill oneself

- giving away special possessions

- saying that nothing matters anymore

If more than one of these behaviors is evident, the risk for depression or suicide is usually greater.

If your friend is talking about suicide, take what he or she says seriously. Listen. If your friend is planning suicide right now, don't leave him or her alone. Don't agree to keep the plans a secret. Be supportive and nonjudgmental. Don't try to handle all the pressure and the situation by yourself. Get help.

Most communities have a suicide hotline listed in the phone book, or you can call the National Hopeline Network at 1-800-SUICIDE (1-800-784-2433). Links for suicide hotlines in the United States are listed at *suicidehotlines.com,* and at Befrienders International for crisis phones in other countries at *www.befrienders.org/talk.htm.* These hotlines can help you help your friend, or your friend can call directly.

***

Sometimes it's hard work being a good friend. You may be faced with some hard choices, especially if you're thinking about telling an adult about a friend's problem. Your friend might get mad at you, but hopefully that wouldn't last very long. If you think your friend is being abused, is feeling depressed, or is considering suicide, try to help him or her feel less alone. If you're not sure what you can do to help, ask an adult you trust—you may need a little help figuring out how to talk about hard things, too. (Chapter 11 has some suggestions on how to talk about hard things.)

Remind yourself:
"I know that I can't fix everything for my friend—I can just help."

Be sure to get support for yourself, too, because helping others is hard work. Don't get lost in your friend's life by trying to solve all of his or her problems. You still need to take care of yourself. It's sometimes easy to forget about your own boundaries when you see a friend hurting. That's why asking an adult to help can be a good thing—so you don't feel responsible for everything yourself. If you start feeling bad or worrying all the time about your friend—so much that you can't concentrate on anything else—you may be trying to help too much. Maintaining a balance for yourself while helping your friend is better for everyone.

Let It Out

Remember, writing in a journal is a great way to help you figure exactly what's going on in your life and how you feel about it. It's private and usually feels like a safer place to start than talking to someone face-to-face. It's okay if you don't feel ready to do any journaling. Respect yourself and your own pace. Just do those things that you feel ready to do.

Sometimes a friend can help when nobody else feels safe. Really good friends can also help you see things about yourself that you may not see, you may not know how to handle, or you may not want to see.

■ What does being a friend mean to you?

■ What kinds of hard choices have you faced in a friendship?

■ What would you want a friend to do for you if you were being abused, or if you were feeling depressed or suicidal?

Resources

Hotlines

CDC National STD and AIDS Hotline
1-800-227-8922
For more information about the Centers for Disease Control (CDC) and the STD and AIDS hotline, see page 134.

Emergency Contraception Hotline
1-888-NOT-2-LATE (1-888-668-2528)
www.not-2-late.com
This toll-free automated service provides listings and contact information for the five emergency contraception providers nearest you. You can also visit the Web site for information about all forms of emergency contraception.

National Abortion Federation Hotline
1-800-772-9100
www.prochoice.org
Available Monday through Friday from 8 A.M. to 10 P.M. and Saturday and Sunday from 9 A.M. to 5 P.M. EST, this hotline offers nonbiased information about pregnancy and abortion, clinical referrals, and a listing of funding resources. Visit their Web site for further information on all of the personal, financial, and legal issues involved with abortion.

National Center for Victims of Crime Hotline
1-800-FYI-CALL (1-800-394-2255)
For more information about the National Center for Victims of Crime and the services they provide, see page 135. The referral line is available Monday through Friday from 8:30 A.M. to 8:30 P.M. EST.

National Life Center Pregnancy Hotline
1-800-848-LOVE (1-800-848-5683)
www.nationallifecenter.com
This 24-hour hotline offers free counseling to girls and women confused or concerned about an unplanned pregnancy. Offering confidential, nonjudgmental, and respectful guidance and counseling, the hotline can also provide referrals to one of over 3,500 nationally associated health and counseling centers.

National Runaway Switchboard Hotline
1-800-621-4000
To learn more about the National Runaway Switchboard and their hotline, see page 135.

Books

Back on Track: Boys Dealing with Sexual Abuse by Leslie Bailey Wright and Mindy Loiselle (Brandon, VT: Safer Society Foundation, 1997). This workbook for boys and young men helps victims recognize and deal with feelings and points the way toward support and possible solutions for feeling better. Real-life situations, guided exercises, and writing opportunities aid healing and promote positive feelings toward the future.

In Love and in Danger: A Teen's Guide to Breaking Free of Abusive Relationships by Barrie Levy (Seattle: Seal Press, 1997). Dating violence among teens is at an all-time high. Learn how to escape dangerous relationships that take a physical and emotional toll. Covering male and female perspectives in both opposite-sex and same-sex relationships, this book offers practical advice for avoiding and escaping abusive partners.

Shining Through: Pulling It All Together After Sexual Abuse by Mindy Loiselle and Leslie Bailey Wright (Brandon, VT: Safer Society Foundation, 1997). This book, written for girls and young women, addresses the feelings that occur after abuse, offering support and coping strategies that are practical and respectful. Find information about self-esteem, body image, relationships, and other helpful advice for moving past abuse.

The Struggle to Be Strong: True Stories by Teens About Overcoming Tough Times edited by Al Desetta and Sybil Wolin (Minneapolis: Free Spirit Publishing, 2000). Read about 30 young people who have faced some of life's most difficult challenges and, with effort and determination, persevered. Seven keys to remaining resilient help you to carry these lessons into your own life.

When Nothing Matters Anymore: A Survival Guide for Depressed Teens by Bev Cobain (Minneapolis: Free Spirit Publishing, 1998). Find out the causes and types of depression and the different kinds of treatment, how they help, and how to stay healthy. This book provides survival tips, resources, and true stories from others who have dealt with depression.

Web Sites

Mental Help Net
www.mentalhelp.net
This is a one-stop site for information and advice on every conceivable mental health topic. Find a glossary of mental health terminology, listings of symptoms, and current information on psychological issues. Also available are helpful resources for taking positive steps to feeling better, including the opportunity to find a therapist or treatment facility in your area.

National Youth Violence Prevention Resource Center
www.safeyouth.org
This site offers information on a variety of topics, including dating violence, substance abuse, and mental health issues. Geared specifically to teens, the site also provides places to look for more help.

Teen Advice Online
www.teenadviceonline.org
It sometimes seems that problems are unique to an individual and that dis-cussing them with others will do little or no good. This site, however, is proof that people are not alone in their problems. Written by and for teens, the site offers helpful information and the opportunity to confidentially pose ques-tions to a network of peer advisors.

TeenSpace @ The Internet Public Library
www.ipl.org/div/teen
This virtual library offers information on many of the difficult issues facing teens today. Click on "Issues and Conflicts" for information about abuse, counseling services, family relationships, law matters, and more. The main teen site acts as a gateway to sites and information about health, the Internet, and more.

Organizations

Centers for Disease Control and Prevention (CDC)
National Center for HIV, STD, and TB Prevention
Division of Sexually Transmitted Diseases
1600 Clifton Road
Atlanta, GA 30333
1-800-227-8922
www.cdc.gov/std
The Centers for Disease Control and Prevention offer information on all aspects of health. The contact information above, however, will put you in touch with STD and HIV information specifically. The hotline listed features access to counselors and health professionals who answer health inquiries 24 hours a day. General information about STDs and clinical referrals are also available.

International Child Abuse Network (Yes I CAN)
7657 Winnetka Avenue, Suite 155
Canoga Park, CA 91306
1-888-224-4226
www.yesican.org
This organization works to keep the topic of child abuse in the news and on people's minds with the intention of decreasing its occurrence. Write, call, or visit their Web site for articles, statistics, and resources about abuse. Online visitors will find the experiences of abuse survivors and the opportunity to share their own messages or questions with professionals in the field. The phone number listed above is not a crisis line; if you need to report abuse, call 1-800-422-4453.

National Center for Victims of Crime (NCVC)
2000 M Street NW, Suite 480
Washington, DC 20036
1-800-FYI-CALL (1-800-394-2255)
www.ncvc.org
This center helps crime victims locate crisis intervention, counseling, and support services in their area. These referral services are accessible via the center's hotline, available Monday through Friday from 8:30 A.M. to 8:30 P.M. EST, and at their Web site. Their Web site also features articles, statistics, and helpful information for staying safe.

National Runaway Switchboard
3080 North Lincoln Avenue
Chicago, IL 60657
1-800-621-4000
www.nrscrisisline.org
If you're not safe at home, or if you're consistently put in situations that leave you feeling bad or uncomfortable, it may be time to leave (though perhaps only temporarily). The National Runaway Switchboard can help you decide if it is the right step for you. Call the national hotline listed above 24 hours a day or visit their Web site for information, support, and referrals that can help you stay safe and start feeling better.

Part 3 Your Healing Journey

CHAPTER 14

What Does It Mean to Heal from Abuse?

You begin healing from abuse as soon as you start talking about your experiences, maybe even when you begin thinking about making changes in your life. Healing starts by beginning to think about yourself in a different way than before—feeling more empowered, feeling that your opinion matters, feeling that you matter.

Healing means change. Although change can feel scary, it's also exciting, kind of like the feeling you get on a roller coaster—scary but fun at the same time. When you start making changes, you may notice sensations similar to the extremes of a roller-coaster ride—remember that there are many people around you who want to help. Part of your healing process may include learning how to ask for help in a way that feels okay to you. You may begin to learn many new things about yourself as you heal. Your healing process is a starting point for changes within yourself. That's exciting, too.

> I thought talking would be really hard, but my counselor was easy to talk to. She really understood. It felt like letting go of all the bad stuff.
> —CHELLE, 15

Healing is a very individual process that can even vary for you at different times in your life since you're still growing and developing—emotionally, socially, and psychologically, if not physically. Your needs are different from when you were 10, or what they'll be in a few years. Being different than you were a few years ago, or even a few months ago, is part of the reason that you've been able to explore making changes in your life now.

What Is the Healing Process?

Some people compare the healing process to the layers of an onion or to a wave. Both of these analogies refer to "revisiting" an issue. With the wave, you may be carried closer to the shore, only to be pulled back out. There's a cyclical nature to being carried by a wave, just like with healing. You may feel as if you're moving forward for a while and then find yourself being pulled back into issues you thought were solved. That's because you understand the issues differently as you get older.

> Sometimes I still get mad about the abuse, 'cause healing takes a long time. Just when I think I'm over all those old feelings, something makes me think about them again.
>
> —Reggie, 17

The process of healing is sometimes compared to peeling back the layers of an onion. Healing requires that each individual layer be examined, that you work through the layers of hurt feelings, thoughts, and memories. That's part of the reason healing can take a long time, because your experiences can affect you differently at each layer or developmental level within yourself.

Remind yourself:
"I care about myself enough to do the hard work of healing."

Healing for people who were abused as young children can take various forms. The healing process may begin soon after the abuse stops, or may not begin until later on—sometimes even years after the abuse stopped. Later, they may begin to think about what happened in a different way. Understanding what being abused means can be a shock that brings back all the old feelings with the emotional understanding. So, healing can occur long after the abuse has stopped, or it can begin right away when the abuse stops.

Everybody heals differently from abuse. Your individual process of healing will depend on a number of things:

- your age at the time of the abuse
- your relationship with the abuser
- whether you're male or female
- if you knew the abuser before the abuse
- how long the abuse lasted
- how often it happened
- the severity and type of abuse (whether it was physical, emotional, sexual, neglect, or some combination)
- your support system
- individual differences about you
  - personality
  - coping styles
  - resiliency or ability to bounce back from hard things
  - family beliefs, behaviors, and patterns (for example, if people believed you or if talking is okay in your family)

Your healing process may take more time and feel harder, depending on what your experiences have been. Healing can be more challenging if you were younger when the abuse started. If the abuse happened for a long time, it may be harder to tell the difference between what types of behavior are okay and what aren't. Learning new boundaries is important, but often hard when abuse has been a large part of your life. The experience of abuse can begin to feel normal if it's been happening a long time. Or when abuse begins at a young age, you're more likely to accept it as normal—partly because you just don't know what else life looks like. Thinking that any kind of abuse is normal can make it harder to unlearn the behaviors, feelings, and thoughts associated with the abuse. With sexual abuse, the abusive behaviors can come to seem like a form of affection, even though they're not. Behaviors, thoughts, and feelings learned through being physically or emotionally abused can teach you unhealthy ways to control yourself or others. Healing will require you to readjust your views of yourself, the world, and others.

Adjusting your view of yourself and the world is a critical part of any healing process, but it's also hard. There's an old saying that suggests anything done well is worth the effort, and the same is true of the healing process for abuse. You'll feel more alive, confident, and generally happier if you put effort into your healing, especially if you've been denying the impact of the abuse.

Denial is a way that some people protect themselves from hard feelings. Most people are not aware that they are in denial. By definition, being in denial prevents you from recognizing things as they really are. People often deny their own harmful behaviors, painful feelings, or negative thoughts about things that seem too awful to be real. If you're in denial, people who are trying to help you may strongly encourage you to hear things that seem hard to hear. You might react by becoming angry because what they're suggesting seems too ridiculous. Try to keep in mind these people care about you, and that's why they may be pushing you in your healing process. Listen to what they suggest, and explore your own feelings as honestly as you can.

I didn't even know what denial was, but I was in it—that's for sure. I told everybody—including myself—that being abused didn't bother me. But whenever I got angry at somebody, I'd just start punching. I never used to do that. My counselor helped me see it was exactly what my mom did to me. Wow, did that ever open my eyes. Denying how bad the abuse hurt was like lying to myself. Now that I'm starting to work through how much I really hated being abused, I am beginning to make choices for myself. I'm not letting my hidden feelings control me because of my denial.

—SHARRELLE, 18

Staying in denial is a form of self-protection, but it comes at a high price. Usually it means you're living a limited life—not feeling things as fully, not allowing yourself to try new things, being afraid of others' reactions to you. Moving past your denial can lead to a new kind of freedom. Freedom never comes easy, but it's always worth the effort. Your healing process will liberate you from pain, hurt, and bad feelings.

> Some days I hated going to see my therapist, but now I'm glad I stuck with it.
>
> —STEVE, 18

Remind yourself:
"Healing may take a long time and may feel uncomfortable at first."

What About the Saying "Different Strokes for Different Folks"?

This funny phrase from the 1970s suggests that everybody has different needs and different things that make them feel good about themselves. The same is true of the healing process. Although some aspects of healing are fairly universal, the way that each person goes through the process can be strikingly different. Here are some of the universal tasks of healing:

- talking about what happened in a way that provides for emotional release

- letting go of self-blame

- resolving anger

- seeing yourself as important, capable, and strong

- building skills to say "no"

- building skills to identify what you need and what you don't need
- setting boundaries
- setting your own priorities
- learning to trust your own judgment and instincts
- learning to trust others
- learning what you like and don't like
- learning to love yourself

Although healing can be a really challenging process, it leads to some wonderful aspects of life and of yourself. Some of the things you can look forward to include feeling better about yourself, having more choices, enjoying fun activities that other people your age do, and not worrying about the abuse. Sometimes, focusing on the opportunities that you're making for yourself can help you push through the hard parts.

So, how do people get to those new places in their lives and within themselves? Again, healing is an individual process, one that depends on your own readiness to change. Don't feel pressured to go faster than what feels right for you, but be open to making changes. You may be ready to start healing before the abuse has even ended, or you may not be ready until years after it stopped. There's no right or wrong way to heal. Finding the way that works best for you may take a little bit of time—like an experiment—so try to be patient if your first attempts for healing don't work just right.

I had to take a break from therapy for a while— right after the court case.

—RASHEIN, 16

So what choices might you have for healing? Professional therapy or counseling is the best choice, if that's available to you. If you're not sure how to get therapy for yourself, ask one of the adults around you who you trust. If Child Protective Services has been involved, ask them about the options available in your community. There are people right at your school who can help. Some schools have social workers or crisis counselors whose job it is to work with students. It's important to remember that healing is hard, but even harder if you try to go through the process alone. Be assured that there are people who want to help you.

More intensive services are available through an inpatient or day treatment program at a hospital or clinic. Although neither of these is usually the first approach for healing, they're available if problems become more serious, like having suicidal thoughts or hopeless feelings that make you want to give up. (See pages 128–129 in Chapter 13 for more on these issues.)

Even though working with a therapist is recommended, individual efforts at healing can be helpful if a therapist isn't available, or in addition to working with a therapist. For example, you can do the journaling exercises in this book on your own. However, take some precautions so that you don't become overwhelmed by your feelings, thoughts, or memories without support. Create a safety plan—like having someone you can call or talk to almost any time—if you're going to be doing any work on your own. You might be surprised by the intensity of your feelings once you begin looking at your honest reactions to the abuse. That kind of surprise isn't easy to manage on your own, no matter how strong you feel. That's why working with a therapist to learn how to deal with these strong reactions during your healing process is recommended.

Here are some activities you can do on your own to begin your healing process:

- drawing

- journaling

- writing therapeutic letters (see page 175)

- reading this book or others that provide personal accounts of abuse and healing

- visiting Web sites about healing (see the resources sections in this book; also see pages 66–67 in Chapter 7 for information on chatrooms)

Drawing, painting, and sculpting are wonderful outlets when words seem to fail you. You can express feelings without even knowing what you think about your experiences, so artwork may be very helpful during the early stages of healing. Creating artwork can help you move toward being able to realize the impact of the abuse on your self-image and your view of others. The creative process is very powerful in that way, but that power can feel overwhelming if you push yourself too far on your own.

> Writing poems helped me get rid of my pain, and made me feel like there was something I was good at.
> —KRISTEN, 14

Journaling is another way to focus on your thoughts and feelings about the abuse. A journal can also be used to focus on positive things, like goals for yourself or good things that are happening at school or with friends. Until you can begin working with a therapist, you may want to use your journal for these more positive things, to build up your self-esteem, confidence, and to feel better about yourself. Turn to pages 4–5 to learn more about using this powerful tool.

How Does a Family Heal?

Abuse affects the whole family—whether or not the abuser was a family member. Everyone must adjust to the idea of what happened and come to understand its deep psychological impact. They must learn how to cope with it in healthy ways and how to deal with one another.

If the Abuser Was a Family Member

As people work on healing from abuse, they usually deal with issues of trust, especially if the abuser was a family member. In these cases, disclosure (whether it's direct or indirect) affects everybody's relationships in your family. It's important to remember that it's not your responsibility to take care of anyone else's feelings about and reactions to the abuse.

Feeling nervous or uncomfortable may be part of the initial changes in your family relationships after the abuse is disclosed. There will probably be changes in your living arrangements or at least in who's living in your house. Those changes are hard and may make you feel angry, guilty, sad, afraid, or all these things at once.

You may wonder how your family is going to manage financially if one parent leaves the home. Although it's logical to think about those things, it's not your job to worry about that. The abuse wasn't your fault, and none of the changes that occur after the abuse stops are your fault either. Other family members may make you feel guilty about changes in the family, even if they don't do it on purpose. That's part of the reason it's so important to have some support for yourself outside the family.

Why Deal with This Now?

Although it may seem easier to just put the abuse behind you and not do any work on healing right now, the situation is a little like getting a bad scrape—like when you used to fall off your bike as a little kid and get gravel in the scrape. You probably didn't leave all the dirt and gravel in the wound—if you had, it never would have healed, right? That's kind of like the healing process. If you leave all the hurt feelings, negative thoughts, and bad memories inside you, they tend to fester like a wound that has dirt and gravel in it. You have to clean it out and let it heal, or the infection keeps getting worse. Doing the hard work of healing now helps you avoid problems later.

There are many ways that family members can discount your feelings and experiences. Maybe it feels as if your family doesn't believe you about the abuse. Maybe it feels like they blame you for changes that have happened in the family. Maybe they act like the abuse didn't happen or it's no big deal. These are all ways that others discount your feelings and experiences. In some ways, that's a continuation of abusive behaviors. Although these may not be intentional on their part, these are issues that your family members need to get help for. Your family may need help dealing with some of these issues, separate from your issues, in their own counseling or therapy. Your family members need to take responsibility for their own feelings and healing process, just like you are for yourself.

Sometimes family members blame themselves for what happened to you. They may feel really sad or guilty about that, and probably don't know how to make up for it. Although they really can't make up for what happened, you'll probably want to talk with them about your feelings at some time. Having a good relationship with family members will require work from everyone, but it will get better.

> It felt like everybody in my family wanted me to get over it really fast. My friends helped me figure out how to tell them I just didn't trust them yet.
> —MICAH, 17

Every family heals differently, just like every individual has different needs in healing. You know your family better than anyone else, so you probably have some good ideas about the challenges for yourself and your family in healing from this abuse. For example, if there's a history of abuse in your family, how it was dealt with before will probably influence how your family tries to deal with it now—if that was by pretending it didn't happen, that's probably what will happen again. Individual, ethnic, and cultural differences also can affect how your family heals. For example, do males in your family have a strong leadership role? Those expectations may make a father who abuses his children feel invincible and make mothers, grandmothers, and daughters less likely to speak up. Boys in a family with a dominating father, or in a family with "macho" expectations for males, may feel they can't speak up because they're afraid of being ridiculed. On the other hand, a strong father who is not abusive can be a great source of support.

In some families, there may be strong women who support children and expect abusers to be responsible for their behaviors. In others, strong women may feel able to abuse their children without any consequence. Boys in these families may feel embarrassed that they were controlled by a woman, and that may make talking about it and healing from it hard. Girls might think they have no choice but to follow their mother's example and become a "tough girl," even if that isn't how they really feel. Outside support and intervention are necessary in all these examples to help families make healthy changes following abuse. Families often get stuck in patterns while abuse is happening and may need someone outside the family to facilitate change and healing.

If the abuse has been happening in a family for a long time— maybe even back to parents and grandparents, healing might be more than just hard. In families like this, the person who's been abused might be the only one who wants a change. The rest of the family might be in denial. Healing for the whole family may not happen in those situations. It might be healthy to look to other supportive adults who can help be there for you.

If the Abuser Wasn't a Family Member

When the abuser was someone outside of your family, learning how to trust other people or feel safe in your daily life will be hard. You may feel uncomfortable wherever the abuse happened—for example, at home, at school, or in a park. You may also feel more suspicious of others, questioning the motives of strangers and your ability to be safe with people—those you know and don't know. These kinds of feelings are a challenge whether the abuse has been going on for a long time, or for a shorter period of time.

Your family may be experiencing some of this uncertainty, too, and may try to protect you by hovering over you or becoming more restrictive with your curfew or time with friends. Your parents may need to relearn how to trust your independence again, as you're learning to do the same. It's probably not your trustworthiness that's the issue, but your parents will be concerned about your safety.

Your family will probably be angry with the person who abused you and may push for legal consequences or other action to hold the abuser accountable for what happened. You may or may not be comfortable with their choices or need for action or revenge, or you may agree with them fully. If you feel supported by their actions, that's great. If not, you may need support from outside your family, too.

***

Deciding to take care of yourself by working on healing is really, really healthy, but it's also really, really, hard. You will work at your own pace. As you heal, you will feel stronger. Your strength in surviving the abuse will help you heal as well. Many people say they feel stronger and happier after overcoming big obstacles like abuse, but it takes time. Be patient with yourself. You're well on your way to feeling better about yourself, by deciding to do what you need to do so you can heal.

Remind yourself:
"I'm looking forward to feeling better about myself, almost excited."

Let It Out

Remember, writing in a journal is a great way to help you figure exactly what's going on in your life and how you feel about it. It's private and usually feels like a safer place to start than talking to someone face-to-face. It's okay if you don't feel ready to do any journaling. Respect yourself and your own pace. Just do those things that you feel ready to do.

- What do you need from your family to start healing?
- Describe the kinds of healing that feel best to you right now.

CHAPTER 15

Who Can Help with My Healing?

Deciding who can help with your healing may seem difficult at first. After all, you've never been through something like this before and don't know how people will react to what's happened—or how helpful they can be. That's okay. You don't need to have all the answers now. Healing is a process and you can't know what kind of help you'll need for the stages that are unfolding in front of you. Your needs may change as you go along. Still, it's helpful to consider the different sources of support that may be available to you.

> I didn't know how hard asking for help would be, but talking got easier once I started.
>
> —BRIANNA, 13

In Chapter 9, you created a list of people in your support network. Refer back to that list now. Although you may not feel comfortable turning to each of these individuals for help with this part of your healing process, reviewing the list may help you think about:

- what kinds of help you do want and need now
- what types of professionals might be able to help
- what informal kinds of support you have

How Can You Feel Safe?

When your experience shows you that the world isn't such a safe place, you have a huge task of adjustment facing you. You have to figure out how to feel safe and keep on going. You need the support of other people in your healing process, and the good news is that there are caring and trustworthy people around who want very much to help you. Yet, you may not feel comfortable accepting or asking for support. That's understandable because trust is slow to rebuild after being abused. It may be hard to trust others or to talk about what you need. You won't know exactly what you need, but getting used to asking is part of the healing process. Beginning to feel okay about asking for help and sharing parts of yourself with others—while still feeling safe—will make a big difference in your life. You may feel less anxious or less worried as you begin to let others help you. Asking for help and talking about what has happened to you means you don't have to carry the whole burden yourself anymore. That will make a positive difference for you. You won't have to do all the hard work of healing alone. Working with a therapist or a counselor from school or family services will help you figure out what's next for you.

Remind yourself:
"I can find the kind of help that's best for me."

Who Should You Turn To?

Turning to professionals and other people in your support network is different at different times in your healing journey. The help you receive after you first talk about what's happened and during the legal process will probably be more fact-based than later in your healing. Your focus during the early parts of telling and the legal parts may be to stay strong and stay connected with trusted adults. It's important to begin to let others help support you. You don't have to do it all alone anymore. Your emotions will probably vary from day to day, and a therapist can help you express them safely and learn how to cope with them—important steps as you begin to heal. Talking later during the healing process may feel more emotional as you are able to become more honest with yourself and others about how painful the abuse has been. As you work with others, it's important to acknowledge how much the abuse has hurt. That acknowledgment will help you let go of some of the pain from the abuse.

> Finding out I could talk about my feelings and not get hit felt like being free.
>
> —Jamal, 15

You need to be able to talk about your experiences, but not feel forced to talk sooner than you're ready to at any given time. Find others who can give you support and freedom to discuss your feelings, while respecting how hard it is to talk about what happened. If it feels like somebody is pushing too hard, ask that person to stop.

Therapist/Counselor

Professional therapy or counseling is the best place for open conversations and skill rebuilding to occur. It will also be important to talk about your feelings in those open conversations. You might think it would be too hard to talk to someone you don't know very well about such personal things, but sometimes that can make it easier to talk—especially once you've established a comfortable, trusting, working relationship with a therapist or counselor. The therapeutic relationship is not emotionally charged in the same way that family relationships are. Although feeling close to your therapist is important in being able to trust and work with them, you don't have to worry about your therapist getting angry with you, or making you feel bad in other ways. Since a relationship with a therapist is different than relationships in your family, you will be better able to discuss painful and sensitive experiences without the strain of trying to protect or please significant adults (like your parents).

You may be worried about how other people might react if they hear what happened to you. Family members won't know what you're talking about in therapy, unless you tell yourself. Your therapist or counselor has a confidential relationship with you. Although there are some instances when that confidentiality may be broken, it is only in legal cases or to make sure you're safe. Your therapist will talk with you about these kinds of issues at the very beginning of therapy.

Finding a Therapist or Counselor: Making the decision to talk with a counselor or therapist about your feelings and experiences is an important first step in healing, but you may not know how to go about finding one. Your school counselor's office is an easy place to start, although counselors at most schools aren't able to continue working with you about abuse for a long period of time. The school counselor, Child Protective Services, an attorney involved with your case, or maybe a teacher, coach or other trusted adult can help you find a therapist in your community.

Sometimes you can find a counselor through your religious community or other community groups, like a voluntary action center, or even through Child Protective Services. Although it's different in every community, there are often counselors who will volunteer their services and time to work with people who don't have insurance or are unable to pay for sessions. State programs are also available to help pay for counseling services in some cases. A good way to find a counselor or therapist is to ask some of the people who helped you when you told or during the investigation and legal parts of the process. These people may even arrange counseling for you.

You can also talk with your doctor or ask friends for any recommendations.

I knew my friend Lisa saw a therapist, so I asked her for her name and phone number. That felt a whole lot better than just going in to see anybody.
—ALICIA, 16

Questions to Ask a Potential Therapist or Counselor

You need to be comfortable with a counselor or therapist in order to work with the person about these sensitive issues. Here are some good questions to ask on a first visit:

- What ways do you use to help clients deal with trauma and abuse?

- How long do you usually work with clients who have been abused?

- What about confidentiality? What do you need to tell my parents about our counseling sessions?

- How do you feel about working with people who have questions about their sexual orientation?

- How do you feel about working with me?

To find more advice on choosing a counselor or therapist, look for books on the subject—at your library, from your school counselor, or from the workers who have been helping since you started talking about your abuse experiences. A Web site provided by the American Psychological Association may also help with choosing a therapist (*helping.apa.org/brochure/index.html*).

How They Can Help: Many therapists and counselors have lots of experience working with people who have been abused. They have many "tools," or techniques, to help you during your healing process. They can help you find the tools that will work best for you and the issues you're dealing with. As you work on healing, they can help you:

- understand the impact of your abuse and its possible repercussions

- express emotions (for example, anger, sadness, or fear)

- empower yourself to regain a sense of control

- give yourself permission to let go of certain angry responses

In the safety of therapy, you can begin to explore frightening memories and overwhelming feelings, such as sadness or anger. Strong feelings can often mimic the experience of abuse, leaving some people feeling hopeless and helpless to bring about change. When they encounter these kinds of feelings outside of the support of therapy, they may become out of control. However, when such feelings arise during therapy or counseling, the therapist can guide you in finding ways to deal with such strong feelings and release them in a healthy and safe way. The person can also help you begin to understand how the feelings relate to the abuse.

Remind yourself:
"I can find a safe place to work through my feelings."

Support Groups

A support group is made up of people your age who have experienced similar life challenges. It's a good idea to participate in one in addition to going to individual therapy. A group meets on a regular basis—ranging from weekly to once or twice a month—to provide emotional support to each other. Support groups for teens are often facilitated by professionals or by an adult from the community. The word "facilitate" is used, rather than "lead," because the purpose of a support group is for members to share their experiences, coping skills, and perceptions in order to provide support for other group members. These groups are not "led" by an adult in the traditional sense.

A group can provide a very positive experience when all members feel supported; however negative experiences can occur as well if any one member becomes overwhelmed by his or her feelings. Other members of the group may also become overwhelmed at this time. Strong feelings can trigger memories, thoughts, or emotions in other group members just as they do in you. Before joining a support group, check with your therapist or counselor to determine if you both agree that the timing is right in your healing process. Your therapist will have information about appropriate groups for you.

> I never thought I could talk in a group, but I really like hearing how everybody else feels about stuff—and almost everybody feels like me.
>
> —JULIA, 14

Helping others is often a very powerful part of healing. Although you may not be ready now, you may want to give back to others at some point. For some people, giving back and supporting others is a way of making sense of abuse. It can also help you feel less alone and isolated.

Family

How your family helps you heal will depend on many different things, including:

- what your relationships were like before, during, and after the abuse

- who the abuser was and what kind of relationship you and your family members had with him or her

- what you need to feel better about yourself

You may have to know more about what you need for yourself before you can ask your family for help. It might feel hard to ask for what you need, because you may still be afraid of what they'll do if you're honest with them. You're probably still uncertain about others' reactions. Think about the different factors involved in your experience of abuse and how that might affect your healing process. Your therapist or the therapist working with your family can help you figure this out.

> My mom tried to totally make up for the abuse by being all up in my business. I asked her to back off, and she did.
>
> —MABLE, 16

What are your fears about what others think about you in relation to the abuse?

■ Are you afraid they don't believe you?

■ Do you fear that they're angry with you for talking about the abuse?

■ Do you fear that changes in the family are your fault?

■ Do you fear that your relationships with family members are forever changed?

■ Do you fear that you may abuse others?

■ What do you need to feel better about yourself in light of these fears?

How family members react to you depends on their own experiences as well. For example, if others in your family have been abused themselves, you'll probably feel their support more quickly and maybe more strongly than is comfortable for you at first. Depending on what kind of healing family members have gone through themselves, their responses and support to you may feel really good, too distant, or too close. If you have support from a therapist or counselor—someone outside your family—it would be a good idea to talk with them about how family relationships are feeling (for example, good, suffocating, angry, confusing).

If the therapist is aware of how you're feeling, he or she can help you with your feelings and help you figure out a way to improve family relationships, when that is possible. The therapist may be able to talk with them or set up a family session to work on communication or feelings of guilt and blame. While it can be helpful to wait for this until you feel ready, your family members or therapist may push for a meeting before you feel completely ready. It's also important to know that when abuse occurs in families, relationships may be so damaged or strained that reaching an ideal point may not be possible. Healing the relationships with family members will be hard work—that's why it's important to have your therapist there to help. Talk to your therapist, or a trusted adult, about your feelings, perceptions, and hopes for the healing process. Working out your goals with someone else will feel easier with their support and guidance.

One of the hard parts about working things out with your family is that things may not go the way you want them to. People in your family may not have been able to deal with their own feelings about the abuse yet, making it hard to work on relationship changes. It's helpful to know what you want from your family for your own healing but also important to understand that you may not get that response from them. This is another reason why working with a therapist is important, to help you cope with unexpected reactions from family members.

Friends

How you feel about talking to your friends about the abuse is going to vary, based on how close you feel to them, if you've spoken with them about your feelings and experiences, and even how large or small your community is. For most teens, friends are a really strong source of support. Yet you may feel too embarrassed about what happened to feel comfortable talking with them. This is especially true for guys, who often like to see themselves as too strong to be abused in any way. Sexual abuse offers another challenge for guys talking about abuse because so many perpetrators are male, making you question your own sexuality, and fearing that your friends might wonder the same thing. Even if the abuser was female, it wasn't right, no matter how "cool" people think it is to have sex. Girls sometimes have a hard time talking about abuse because of their strongly ambivalent feelings toward the abuser and themselves. Both boys and girls struggle with blaming themselves for what's happened, and that can be another obstacle to talking with friends.

Friends can be really helpful while you're struggling with all these changes, but it's important to remember to keep a balance between keeping your friends as friends and using them as a therapist. If you find yourself talking to lots of people about your abuse, that's probably a good sign that you need to talk with your therapist about these things. You may feel really distant from your friends, because your life seems so different from theirs. No matter how alike or different you feel from them, reaching out to your friends will probably help you feel supported. Just remember to have fun with your friends—keep them as friends. If somebody asks you about the abuse, or if you feel hesitant about telling someone, you can just say, "I can't talk about that just yet." You'll be learning how to take care of yourself, and you'll be healing in the process.

Friends can also provide support by helping you have fun. Laughing is healthy. There are proven health benefits from laughing, and being with friends. Healing isn't just about expressing your feelings and releasing bad memories, it's also about learning who you are and living life. Friends are a great resource for those types of explorations, whether they're new or old friends.

Remind yourself:
"It's healthy to laugh."

A Higher Power/Spirituality

This book has talked a lot about trusting your feelings. Some people believe that trusting themselves is a form of spiritual connection. For many people, trusting their faith or spiritual beliefs can provide a strength that feels stronger than other types of support. If you already have connections through a church or spiritual group, that's a good place to look for support. Many spiritual and religious organizations have youth groups that can be supportive in a different way—helping you get connected to activities and other people. Another positive aspect of these organizations is the opportunity for learning healthy coping mechanisms and releases. Any positive activities or coping skills you can learn will help with your healing.

If you're not connected to a church or other spiritual organization, this might a time to explore that. For most teens, learning about other perspectives, faiths, and spiritual approaches is a part of normal development. It may feel good to you to know that you're doing things that other people your age are also doing. Feeling part of a group in that way is another type of support. Spirituality and faith can be strong sources of support in many different ways for different people.

People who have been abused by someone in a religious organization may not feel so comfortable with spirituality or religion.

For these people, spirituality or their familiar religious place may not feel like a source of support. Chapter 7 talks about what happens if you were abused by someone in your religious community.

Pets or Objects

At various points in your healing journey and life in general, you might feel like you need someone to listen to you. Although it may seem silly at first—especially because of all the serious ways to obtain support—pets can be a wonderful source of support. You may already know this from your own personal experiences. If you haven't experienced this yourself, think about how you feel when you see a puppy on the street. Most people smile when they see a puppy or are amused by pets at the zoo. That's a connection that happens on an emotional level. Studies show that animals and people benefit from touch. The simple act of petting an animal can help you feel better. The connection between people and animals is one of unconditional support. You don't even have to talk about what's going on; you can just feel loved and supported.

Maybe you could use this time in your life to consider getting involved with animals, especially if you don't have a pet of your own. Local animal shelters, Humane Societies, and pet therapy programs for preschools and senior centers always need volunteers. Again, helping others can be valuable in healing yourself—it's an amazingly powerful experience.

Although the strength gained from special mementos and objects is not the same as a relationship with people or animals, you may have objects or things that are comforting to you. For example, you might have pictures, souvenirs, or stuffed animals given to you by friends or family. Places can also be comforting, and might include special places around town that remind you of times when you have felt good about yourself, or when you have felt strong, safe, and supported. These kinds of feelings will help you heal. The power of these objects or places for your healing is in the reactions you have toward them. What memories do these special places evoke in you? What strong feelings do you notice when you look at certain pictures? You may also notice that, when you're around some other objects, you have feelings or reactions that are draining or troubling for you. Put those things away, and focus on objects and places that make you feel strong, warm, and powerful. You may even want to carry some of those photos with you when you know you're going to be going through a hard time, or drop by those special places in your neighborhood when you're feeling kind of down.

How Can You Help Others Help You?

Just as you've had to learn how to talk about the abuse with professionals, you may need to figure out ways to talk with friends and family—or at least let them know how you want them to talk with you about it. Again, knowing what you need from others is an important part of healing.

Sometimes it can feel like others don't like you when they don't know how to talk about what's happened to you. Think about a time when something sad or hard happened to somebody else—maybe somebody's grandma died or they lost a pet, or somebody in their family was in a car accident. What did you say or want to say to them? Sometimes it's best just to acknowledge what happened by saying something simple. For example, "I'm sorry about what happened to you. Is there anything I can do?" Just like you, others may not know what they can say or do. Talking to a friend or the school counselor or someone from church—anyone from your support network—about how you feel may help you get the support you need. Any of these people in your support network can act as an intermediary—a go-between—to help you feel supported by others. You can also just ask friends to go do something with you, and that may be enough to help you spend time with a friend, and help them understand that you're still you—although you may be changed by your experiences, you can still have fun and be a friend.

How Do You Say "No" to Offers of Help?

Again, most people don't know how to help you, even though they really care about you. Because of this, some people do nothing and ignore the subject altogether. Other people try to help by doing too much, pushing you to talk when you don't want to, or trying to fix your problems for you. These people aren't mean— just kind of clueless. Though they may be very caring and afraid for you, they don't understand that not everybody needs the kind of help they think is right. Viewing their behavior as well-meaning, but misguided, can help you feel less attacked, suffocated, controlled, or obligated. It's perfectly acceptable and healthy to say no to their offers of help.

Here are some examples of things you can say when talk feels uncomfortable:

- *"Thanks. It's really hard to talk about it too much, but I'd like it if we just hung out."* Suggesting an alternative activity, like just hanging out, can let the person know that you really do like him or her and want to spend time together, but talking just feels uncomfortable. This can help you get the support you need in the way you want. Your friends will want to help you this way.

- *"Mom, it feels like you aren't listening to me. I keep telling you I don't like to talk about it, but you keep asking. I really just need you to be my mom."* This type of request is helping you establish or re-establish appropriate boundaries between your mother (or others) and yourself. Parents don't always know how to be supportive and can push too hard. Another way to think about this is that maybe your mother's behavior just means that she cares about you. If it feels like Mom is just trying to support you or help out, talking with her and telling her how you feel about her constant asking can be a first step in rebuilding your relationship with your mother.

Remind yourself:
"I can say no."

Feeling too close can be as uncomfortable as feeling too alone. It's your perfect right to ask others to respect your privacy when it comes to your decisions not to talk about the abuse just because somebody asks. Being able to say no is another new strength that you're developing.

***

You've accomplished so much on your healing journey. Your strengths and healthy connections with others are probably becoming more evident to you, although you may still be questioning yourself. That's okay—self-doubt is part of the process of self-acceptance, particularly when you've been keeping your true self hidden as a way to survive. Just keep going—learning about what's best for you, turning to your support system when you need help, and becoming more and more yourself.

Let It Out

Remember, writing in a journal is a great way to help you figure exactly what's going on in your life and how you feel about it. It's private and usually feels like a safer place to start than talking to someone face-to-face. It's okay if you don't feel ready to do any journaling. Respect yourself and your own pace. Just do those things that you feel ready to do.

■ Who's in your support network for healing? Revise the list you created in Chapter 9.

■ What kinds of things about the people (or places or pets) in your support network make it easy for you to trust them?

CHAPTER 16

Feelings About Abuse

What do you remember as your first feelings about being abused? You may not remember anything from the first time the abuse happened, especially if it started when you were really young. You might have had a "delayed reaction" after you realized what was going on. That realization may not have even occurred until after you began reading this book, talked to friends, or even saw a movie-of-the-week on TV. Realizing you were being abused may have changed the way you felt about yourself. You may not have felt like the same person anymore.

> I was watching a movie on TV, and I just started bawling. It was about abuse.
>
> —ANNIKA, 16

The things that make it hard to feel okay after recognizing you've been abused are "challenges to recovery." Knowing what some of the common "challenges" are can help you feel better about yourself. Knowing other people feel the same things can help—even though what happened to you wasn't what teens are supposed to experience, how you reacted to what happened is normal. It's common for teens who have been abused to feel:

- angry (at yourself, the abuser, your family who didn't protect you, the world)

- ashamed or guilty, like it was your fault that it happened or didn't stop sooner

- embarrassed because someone might think you're gay or weird

- like your parents don't care enough about you because they haven't acted like parents

- bad that you couldn't protect yourself

- like everybody knows what happened to you

- scared that the abuse will happen again or that you'll be blamed

- different or more grown-up than your friends because of what's happened

- like you've lost part of yourself or your childhood

- like your life will never be the same

- like you can't get clean no matter how many times you shower—a dirty feeling that just won't go away

- worthless or like you just don't matter

- as if you're ugly and nobody else will want to be around you

- sad about losing the connection you had with the abuser— not the bad part, the good part

How Do You Avoid Feelings?

Most of the really hard things about being abused—no matter what kind of abuse it is—have to do with feelings. You can talk yourself into or out of most anything in your head, but it's your feelings—in your heart—that are confusing and hard to understand. You might be unaware of your feelings, or you might notice that you only feel certain things—like just being angry or sad. Because some feelings are so hard, lots of people try to avoid them. But it's really kind of like you're Superman and the feelings are kryptonite—sooner or later, the feelings make you weaker or sicker in one way or another if you ignore them. The feelings will continue to sneak back into your life until you deal with what they're trying to tell you. And you may not even know that some of your thoughts and choices are related to these feelings, at least not at first.

Forgetting

Abuse is such a horrible thing to have happen that people try lots of different ways to forget about it:

- Some do it unconsciously, burying it deep in their minds.

■ Others use drugs or risky behaviors to numb the pain (see Chapter 17).

■ Still others just go about their normal lives, pretending nothing happened.

Yet the feelings don't go away. Avoiding feelings just doesn't work—at least not in the long-term.

Sometimes people "forget" abuse experiences for a period of time, but then the memory is triggered by an external event—a movie or a change in a close relationship. And when the memory resurfaces, it can bring a flood of emotions that are quite upsetting. The image you had of yourself and the world may have become shattered and will no longer feel true. You may feel lost and vulnerable—possibly re-creating some of the helplessness you felt when you were being abused.

You may be frightened and upset because you thought you had worked through these memories and experiences—now they're back. Or perhaps you weren't even aware of the experience before the memory was triggered. Your defense mechanisms—psychological ways of protecting yourself from hurtful things—may have worked so well that you didn't even know you were abused. It's hard to deal with because this new image is so different from what you thought about yourself before the memories. (At such times, it may be good to get help from a counselor or therapist.) Many professionals believe that people deal with their memories when they are ready, and part of being ready is feeling safe—physically and psychologically. Although remembering can be hard, it is an important part of healing, and feeling better about yourself.

> I finally was on a date with Cory. He had seemed so nice. Now, I felt like such a little kid, but I was just too scared—I couldn't do it. He was putting his hands all over me, and it felt like spiders—just like when my cousin abused me. I thought I had forgotten all about it. I wish I had. Now I feel like an idiot, and I remember all this awful stuff.
>
> —JAMIE, 16

What About Dating?

Many teens who have been abused don't feel the same way about dating as other people their age. The thought of being alone with another person may be frightening. Some teens who have been abused may not have thought about the abuse for years or even been aware of what happened until they started dating. Being in a close relationship, especially if it's physical, can often trigger flashbacks or memories of long-forgotten traumas. Our bodies remember more than our minds in some cases. We store memories of sight, hearing, smell, touch, even taste—and these memories can be triggered in various ways. Being held by someone, feeling pressured to have sex when you aren't ready, or even having sex willingly may trigger your memories of abuse. Physical or emotional abuse memories can be triggered in a similar fashion. If someone raises a hand, you may find yourself shielding your face or turning away. If your date calls you a name, even jokingly, it may spark memories of abuse if the words or tone of voice are similar enough to what you experienced when you were being abused.

If the thoughts of abuse haven't been conscious, this process of suddenly remembering can be frightening. You may find yourself flooded by memories of events or intense feelings from when you were abused. You might feel that you need to flee immediately from the situation or person. If you trust the person you're with and are aware of the abuse, tell that person. People are more likely to be helpful and supportive if they know what's going on. If you're just becoming aware of your experiences, use your journal to help you record these new perceptions, and then seek support.

Flashbacks

Flashbacks are thoughts and pictures in your head that are often memories of the abuse. They're called flashbacks because they flash you right back to the middle of the abuse and usually make you feel like it is happening all over again. Such memories may make you feel hopeless that life will ever get better, but most of all, it just feels so unfair. If you're experiencing flashbacks, you will need somebody to help you work through the experiences. Old feelings and new feelings get jumbled together during flashbacks. Working with a counselor can help you separate out what you're feeling now from what you felt then, so that you can begin to make sense of your feelings and memories and continue your healing process.

Sometimes when I get bored in math, I just start remembering things—it's almost like I'm getting abused all over again. I have to work really hard to think about something else.

—MARK, 18

Post-Traumatic Stress

Post-traumatic stress disorder, or PTSD, is a group of symptoms or thoughts and feelings associated with a trauma—something bad that happened to you—that continues to bother you. It may feel almost as if you're haunted by memories of the trauma from the abuse. This is similar to what soldiers experience in a war—that's where the description of post-traumatic stress disorder came from. Soldiers were exposed to trauma and awful events that were not part of normal life. When they returned home after war, they sometimes re-lived what they had experienced while fighting—for example, running to hide from something only they can see or crouching down to protect themselves, as if they were back in the war zone. These internal re-creations of past traumatic experiences are flashbacks. The memory is so strong that it feels as if the original experience is happening again. If you have flashbacks, you may feel as if you're back being abused again. The feelings can be so strong that it is almost like it's happening again right now.

Here are some symptoms of post-traumatic stress:

- flashbacks
- nightmares
- repeated memories of the event
- trying to avoid anything associated with the event
- difficulty remembering details of the event
- excessive anxiety

continued ➡

- difficulty feeling safe
- inability to concentrate
- irritability
- feelings of isolation
- trouble expressing or experiencing feelings
- self-mutilating or self-harming behaviors
- trouble falling asleep
- feeling nervous or scared
- extreme psychological or emotional reactions, such as suicidal thoughts or sexual acting out

People who have been abused may have recurrent flashbacks of certain incidents or of the abuser's voice or face, experience nightmares similar to the abuse, or feel excessive anxiety. It may be difficult to feel safe, to concentrate on schoolwork, or in short, to go about living your life. If you're experiencing any of these symptoms, ask a professional for help getting safe and working through your feelings.

Feelings That Keep Coming Back

Why do feelings and memories keep coming back? Largely, it's because the abuse happened when you were still growing and changing. You change as you get older and you continue to understand life, your experiences, and yourself in different ways. It's kind of like the review sessions in math at the beginning of the school year. You may feel like you know all this stuff and don't need to go over it again, but you're a slightly different person than you were the year before, and that means you might understand things differently—better or maybe not as easily. It's the same way with trying to make sense of events in your life. Say you were abused at age six and it stopped when you were eight, or you were abused one time at age 10 or 12—you were very different at each of those ages. You understand and cope with things differently at each age.

As you get older, you may:

■ find yourself getting more and more mad at the abuser

■ understand how wrong it was for the abuser to take advantage of you

■ become aware of what you might have lost as a result of the abuse

■ realize that you might act or feel older than you are because of your experiences

Your feelings toward yourself may also change with time. At 16, what happened at age five can make you feel very sad for that little child inside. Sometimes those feelings of sadness are so strong that they actually scare you away from looking at them. It may feel as though the feelings will overwhelm you. You may feel safer feeling angry instead, but being stuck in any type of feeling doesn't help. Strong feelings can be a way to avoid thinking about what's happened. But as you continue your healing process, you'll need fewer and fewer ways to distract yourself. You'll continue to develop new ways to cope with the memories, thoughts, and feelings about the abuse. These new coping skills will help you feel more confident, capable, and strong.

Remind yourself:
"I don't have to be controlled by what's happened to me."

What About Broken Dreams?

Lots of people who've been abused feel like they have lost part of themselves—maybe physically, or maybe emotionally and psychologically. What that means is that sometimes you have to grieve for the loss of a dream or the loss of how you always saw yourself living. Part of those dreams probably included a "normal," happy family life. Even if your family wasn't "normal," there may have been happy times despite the abuse. Part of what's confusing about abuse—whether the abuser is a family member or not—are the mixed feelings you may have toward the abuser. After the abuse stops, there'll be many positive changes in your life, but there may be special connections between you and the abuser that are lost. You may need to grieve for the loss of that relationship, or at least parts of it, even parts that you thought were good but have since found out weren't so good. If the abuser was a family member who has also worked on healing, you may develop a new relationship with that person. Your feelings and perspective on many different things will certainly change as you heal. Respect your own feelings about these changes in your life.

Remind yourself:
"Although I have had some fears, I'm not letting them stop me. I'm taking care of myself."

What's with These New Fears?

After the abuse stops and you become more aware of your feelings, you may notice new fears and worries. Although these feelings can be strong and may seem overwhelming at times, they'll lose their strength as you continue to heal. Here are some common fears after the abuse stops:

- Everyone knows what happened to me.
- I won't ever be able to trust anyone.
- I won't ever fall in love.
- I won't be able to have kids.
- I don't want to have kids because I may do this to them.
- I'm not worth anything—I'm no good.
- I can't go on.
- No one will want to be with me because I'm "damaged goods."

Everyone Knows

The way you think about yourself and others changes throughout your life, but never more than when you're growing up. For example, when you were younger, you may have believed in magic or in monsters, thinking these things were real. Although you know otherwise now, you thought they were real at one time because of the way your mind worked then. A similar developmental aspect may also be behind the fear that everyone knows what's happened. It's normal to feel like everyone is aware of all the things you're worried about, even though in reality most people around you are thinking about their own worries instead.

I Can't Trust Myself or Anyone Else

You've had to grow up too fast. You've been around people who are selfish and mean. That makes it hard to trust that most people are good. The abuser may have been someone you loved or trusted, and now you doubt your own judgment.

It's important to remember that the abuse is something that never should have happened. At a young age, you experienced something that's extremely difficult and confusing. Being young is part of the reason you may not have been able to make the abuse stop or prevent it from happening. Even so, some people play mind games and convince themselves that they could have stopped it. Such mind games only make you feel bad about yourself. For many different reasons and in many different ways, the person who abused you had control over you then. That's not your fault. You're working to regain control of yourself now—that's what counts! Abusers set up an uneven playing field that worked against you being able to use your own judgment. They trick, coerce, or persuade in order to make you less suspicious and less guarded. They may have also used force or scare tactics. The abuser probably set it up so you never had a chance to question or stop what he or she had planned.

Now that the abuse is over, you may feel suspicious and distrustful of everyone. It will be important for you to find a balance between being suspicious in a way that helps you protect yourself, and being suspicious in a way that makes it hard for you to trust anybody. Although it's hard to know who is safe and who isn't, it may be helpful to work with a counselor or therapist to learn how to find your own way of knowing who is and isn't safe. You may not ever become completely successful at figuring this out (it's hard for most people). There's always a chance someone may fool you (or anyone) into thinking they are a safe person when they are not, but the more you can learn to trust yourself, the less likely that is to happen.

As a result of the abuse, you may:

- be very watchful of changes in people's moods

- pay close attention to nonverbal behavior in others

- want to please other people

- keep your thoughts and feelings to yourself

These behaviors helped you survive the abuse, and they can still be helpful in your life. Yet you may be taking some of the behaviors too far. Start paying attention to how often you behave in these ways—make a "mental note" or keep a record in your journal. As you become more aware of these behaviors, notice the feelings that accompany them. Your feelings may be too strong for what's really happening. You might be overreacting because of the abuse. As you begin to trust your own feelings more, and continue to increase your awareness of these behaviors, you can respond to situations in a different way.

Remind yourself:
"I'm learning how to trust myself and other people—one step at a time."

I Won't Have a "Normal" Life

Many teens who have been abused are afraid that they'll inflict the same kind of pain on someone else or that they won't know how to be in a healthy relationship. For that reason, they say they'll never get in a relationship or have children of their own. At this time in your life, it's too soon to make those decisions. Just the fact that you've picked up this book and are working through your issues and feelings about what happened is a good sign that you'll never do the same thing to anyone else. Sometimes when terrible things happen, the experience can be used to make good choices about going forward in your life.

Many times patterns of behavior and ways of handling feelings get repeated in families. You may be the one to stop the cycle in your family. Try drawing a family outline (listing all the family members you want to include) to see what you know about patterns of abuse in your family. Are there people who are like you, or are you unlike everyone else in your family? You might be the bright spot at the end of an ugly family legacy, but maybe there are good things about people in your family, too. Use the strengths from your family to help you adjust and heal. Find a way to express your feelings about your experiences, your life, and yourself. You can:

- Use your journal to explore your feelings and experiences.

- Draw pictures of your feelings and the changes you're undergoing as you heal.

- Talk about your experience. You may choose to talk to a school counselor, friends, your dog or cat, or maybe you'll just talk into a tape recorder. It may sound like something you would be embarrassed to do, but just talking about things, even if no one responds, can help you feel better. Some teens decide to volunteer to talk to younger kids at school about abuse. The important thing to remember about talking to others is to do it when you feel ready—if it's too soon, you and the people you talk to can feel more confused, instead of better.

I'm Worthless

Some people who have been abused feel like they're no good anymore—like they're "damaged" or "broken," not as good as other people. Even though your logical mind may tell you that's not true, your feelings tell you something very different. Those feelings make you question yourself and think really off-the-wall things about life and yourself. It's hard to learn to trust yourself again—or maybe even trust yourself for the first time, but that will have to happen in order to feel good and move on in life. Part of healing is letting go of these irrational feelings about the abuse and yourself. Sometimes the irrational thoughts are leftover feelings from what the abuser told you or things you told yourself to survive. These things served a purpose then, but now you need different tools to heal.

I Can't Go On

Maybe you fear that you can't go on—that you'll never get over what happened. It may even feel like the person who did this to you is still there, controlling what you do and say and think. Well, that part is over—by reading this book and getting support from others you're making sure that you are much more in charge of your life.

Remind yourself:
"I'm working on regaining control of my life. I like the way it feels!"

***

You've been working hard to feel better. It helps to know that other people have feelings similar to yours about being abused. It can help you feel less alone, and feeling less alone can help you go on with a difficult process. Expressing who you are and figuring out who you want to become are very exciting parts of healing. You're taking control of yourself and your life.

Let It Out

Remember, writing in a journal is a great way to help you figure exactly what's going on in your life and how you feel about it. It's private and usually feels like a safer place to start than talking to someone face-to-face. It's okay if you don't feel ready to do any journaling. Respect yourself and your own pace. Just do those things that you feel ready to do.

■ Make a list of all your feelings, fears, and concerns about being okay. In what ways do you want to be different than you are right now?

■ What dreams do you feel have been lost after the abuse? Are there people who will no longer be in your life because of the abuse? Write down your feelings about these losses—as a journal entry or a therapeutic letter—to help you let go, grieve for the losses, or say good-bye. A therapeutic letter is a letter for your own benefit, not to send to someone else. Sometimes it's easier to say things if you think you're writing to someone besides yourself. Include your feelings, or what is too hard or scary to say face-to-face to the person who abused you or to those you feel didn't protect you. You might even rip up the letter after you've written it, which can be a healthy and safe way to release feelings so they don't stay stuck inside, continuing to make you feel bad.

A therapeutic letter is a great tool to use with your therapist. Be sure to ask for help if the feelings you're expressing in the letter become too strong. You may not be ready to write this letter. Use this tool when, and if, you feel ready to do so. Just like all kinds of healing efforts, a therapeutic letter works well for some people, but not for everybody.

■ Drawing can be another way of symbolizing these losses, or you may come up with some other ideas to express your sadness or anger over these changes. Physical activity can help some people express such feelings, like using a punching bag. Remember, if the feelings get too strong, ask for help in dealing with them.

CHAPTER 17

Your Life Choices

Healing offers you opportunities to make different choices in your life. As you begin this new phase in your life, take some time to examine how you're living your life. Try to look at your choices as either healthy (positive) or unhealthy (negative). Are your choices healthy and life-affirming, or are your choices negative ones that drag you down to a place where you feel heavy or stuck? Do you notice any connections between your choices and the abuse you've been through?

What Are Unhealthy Choices?

Here are some examples of unhealthy choices that leave you feeling out of control.

- drinking
- using drugs
- eating too much or too little
- having sex and/or having lots of sexual partners
- driving dangerously
- fantasizing about suicide
- cutting or burning yourself, or other self-harming behaviors
- avoiding school or other responsibilities
- not taking care of yourself physically
- unhealthy eating habits
- exercising too much
- trying to be perfect
- staying so busy that you never have time for yourself

Why Do Teens Make Unhealthy Choices?

Sometimes it's hard to understand why people make the choices they do. Usually, there's a good reason behind every choice—even if there may seem to be a better way. Teens who have been abused often make unhealthy choices:

■ to find acceptance with a certain group of friends. Often this is the only way they know how to be accepted or receive attention from others—by doing what others want them to do.

■ to dull the pain of abuse or avoid feeling bad. Although these choices may help you avoid bad feelings, it's only temporary. Eventually, they'll catch up with you. Also, when you're making poor choices to avoid feelings, you're not doing the hard work of figuring out who you are. You're still letting old feelings and experiences control you.

■ to feel loved, get attention, or feel "special."

■ because of low self-esteem or feeling worthless. Abusers try to make you feel stupid or helpless—this is one of their tricks to keep the abuse going and you quiet. Continuing to believe things the abuser told you makes you feel bad about yourself, and just keeps the abuser in control—even if he or she isn't a part of your life anymore.

Unhealthy Appetites

Being abused often feels like you're out of control, and one way of coping is to try to control those areas you can. Many people try to do so through their eating patterns or through their sexuality, because these seem like easy things to control. Yet these actions can lead to new problems—a sexual or food addiction, or an eating disorder—and you've lost control when you thought you were regaining it.

Limiting or bingeing food are both ways that people attempt to manage their feelings. Unfortunately, repeating the behavior can become a maladaptive coping skill—in other words, you may get used to limiting food as a way to punish yourself or to cope if you feel anxious. Bingeing is often used as a comfort against anxiety, too, and is sometimes followed by purging—throwing up. Eating large amounts of food, or certain types of food when feeling upset, is also common, and can lead to an unhealthy relationship with food. Unusual eating patterns can become eating disorders over time. Eating disorders can lead to many health problems, including:

- negative effects on metabolism that make normal weight maintenance difficult

- chemical imbalances from unhealthy food choices

- weak bones or poor functioning of internal organs from limited food intake

- damage to the teeth and esophagus from regurgitating

- permanent problems with your weight, metabolism, ability to self-regulate food, or even the ability to find other ways to cope besides using food

Health problems can also result from sexual behavior that's used to distract yourself from your feelings or as a way to get close with someone else. Sex can lead to transmitted diseases, including HIV (the virus that causes AIDS), and pregnancy, not to mention continued feelings of being used or abused by others.

A Closer Look at Eating Disorders

Eating disorders are any type of extreme or unusual eating pattern. Usually these patterns include restricting or controlling food intake in terms of quantity or specific types of food, eating secretly or hiding the amount and types of food being eaten, bingeing or eating a lot of certain kinds of food. People who experience eating disorders often have unrealistic expectations about body image and unrealistic perceptions about their own body size.

People with eating disorders often don't notice their own behaviors. They may be in denial about them. So, as we've discussed with other aspects of healing, it's important for you to get help from a therapist or other professional to help you work through these challenging issues.

Anorexia is a type of eating disorder that often involves restricting food intake, sometimes to the point of starving oneself. It's sometimes necessary for people with severe anorexia to be hospitalized and fed through a tube because they cannot eat. Excessive exercise is often a part of anorexia.

continued ➡

Bulimia is another type of eating disorder, but the relationship with food differs from anorexia. People struggling with bulimia appear to eat normally or less than normal around others; however they have a tendency to binge or eat a lot of one kind of food when alone. Eating what they consider to be a large amount of food will often be followed by purging (throwing up or using laxatives) the food. Purging is unhealthy for your body, particularly if it's through regurgitation (throwing up). Regurgitation of food brings stomach acid into the throat and mouth, and can damage teeth and vital organs. People sometimes use laxatives in an unhealthy way, too.

Overeating. Food can be used as a comfort, or a distraction. Many people gravitate toward eating certain foods when feeling upset, like chocolate or chips. Sometimes it doesn't even matter what foods are enjoyed—the act of eating seems comforting because it numbs difficult feelings. A therapist can help you find other ways to cope besides using food. You can also learn more about eating disorders from the resource listed on page 204.

Alcohol and Other Drug Use

Trying to forget sometimes just doesn't work well enough, so people try to "self-medicate" to avoid their feelings. Yet using alcohol or other drugs often puts you at much greater risk of being abused or hurt. You may be really capable when you're sober, but after drinking or getting high, you can't do as good a job of protecting yourself or even thinking clearly enough to make a choice about what's happening to you. That's one of the effects of using drugs or alcohol—it takes away your choice—kind of like being abused did.

Although using alcohol or drugs may help you forget temporarily, it doesn't work over time. Making changes about drinking or using drugs can be really hard. Many people have trouble quitting on their own. Work with a therapist or counselor to help in making these important changes.

There are also other well-known problems with drinking or using drugs. You might get very sick from drinking too much or from the effects of other drugs. You risk legal problems (especially for underage use), and driving under the influence can result in serious injury or death. Of course, using can also become addictive and result in the drugs controlling your life.

About 4:15 A.M., a guy came over and asked, "Are you drunk? I smell liquor all over you." He laid me on my bed and started to touch me and kiss me. I tried to push him off, but I couldn't. He put his hand on my neck and told me not to move again, and I passed out.

—ROBERTA, 16

Remind yourself:
"Drugs and alcohol won't solve my problems."

Even though the feelings you're trying to avoid may not make you feel good, they will go away (with some work), and you'll end up feeling better after having worked through your feelings. If you choose to continue to use drugs and alcohol to avoid the feelings, they'll always be there, just hidden. And hidden feelings have a way of oozing out that can sometimes be worse than the feelings themselves—even more out of control—possibly causing you to drink or use more and more.

Resources for Alcohol or Drug Problems

Lots of resources are available to help you cope with your need to use. Al-Anon/Alateen, Alcoholics Anonymous, and Narcotics Anonymous all have national and international networks of support groups. The purpose of these groups is to provide support from other people who struggle with similar concerns about alcohol or drug use. Most communities also have AA and NA meetings around town—some just for teens—these can be good resources and another positive source of support for you. Many times, people in AA or NA have also experienced abuse. Look on pages 201–204 for some resources that can help you with alcohol and other drug problems.

Now I know I don't have anything to be ashamed of. He does, and I wish that others will learn from my mistakes. You can't know who to trust. So protect yourself. Don't drink or use drugs at all.

—JENNIFER, 16

Depression

Many people feel depressed after being abused—those types of experiences can leave you feeling worthless, powerless, sad, or unmotivated. These are not choices people make—it's just how you feel. If you have no energy, get angry easily, or don't enjoy much of anything, you may be depressed. Sometimes feelings of worthlessness can lead to suicidal thoughts.

If you're experiencing any of these things, please talk to someone—a friend, parent, counselor—as soon as possible. You can even go to the emergency room of a hospital to get immediate help. If you're at school, telling the school counselor can start the process of getting help. Depressive feelings are a normal reaction to being abused, but the feelings don't have to stay with you forever—but it usually takes support and assistance from others to help you overcome those feelings.

For more severe symptoms or symptoms that have been a problem for weeks or months, professional help or medication are probably necessary tools to help you in working through challenges. Working through feelings about the abuse can help in getting through the depression. The depressive symptoms can make you feel like you don't have any energy, or that life is too hard. It can make you feel all alone, but you don't need to suffer alone—tell someone how you feel, and ask for professional help. Read more about depression and suicide in Chapter 13, and also look at the resources on pages 201–204.

Remind yourself:
"I can choose what kind of life I want to make for myself."

Self-Harming Behaviors

Some people feel so bad about themselves that they actually hurt themselves—by cutting, burning, scratching, hitting, or picking, among other kinds of self-harm. Other people do these things to cope with their feelings or to distract themselves from their pain. The behavior is also called self-mutilation. People who are harming themselves generally try to hide it from others, often by keeping their entire body covered by clothing—even in the summer. If you are harming yourself, working with a professional on these complicated issues is the best way for you to go. Although the support of family, friends, or groups can also be important, they are not likely to have the skills and training necessary to help you make major changes.

Other Risky Behaviors

You may have thought of lots of other risky behaviors while reading through this chapter, or just on your own. Any kind of dangerous or self-destructive behavior can be considered risky, including:

- driving too fast
- getting in fights or threatening others
- choosing dangerous friends or activities, like playing with knives or guns.

If this is what's going on in your life, stop and think about what you're getting out of the behaviors. Do you enjoy the excitement of the risk? Does it make you feel tough or in control? Do you get a sense of belonging or being cool? You may experience short-term reactions from these behaviors that feel good for now, but more problems will probably develop for you if you are making these risky choices. You might even cause permanent damage to yourself or someone else, just because you're trying to avoid your feelings with these behaviors. Challenge yourself to find other talents within yourself that can be exciting and healthy, not self-destructive. You might have to work on finding things you like about yourself as a place to start giving up risky behaviors. Risky behavior is dangerous—talk with a counselor.

Remind yourself:
"I want to make conscious choices for myself and my life."

How Do You Make a Change?

You need to be able to take care of yourself. Maybe you're making unhealthy choices, and you didn't realize they were symptoms of being upset about the abuse. Sometimes your choices are ways that other parts of yourself are telling you there's something wrong. Listen to these other parts of yourself, and make a positive change.

Use the checklist below as a starting place for this part of your healing.

Unhealthy Choices I Want to Get Rid of in My Life

- Drinking alcohol, sometimes until I get drunk

- Getting high on anything so that I don't have to think

- Eating so much that I numb my feelings

- Not eating because I don't deserve to feel good

- Having sex even though it doesn't feel good—at the time, or later

- Scratching or cutting myself so I don't feel any pain

- Driving really fast

- Not caring about school or work

- Fighting with everybody

- Being mean to other people

- Hanging around with people who are making poor choices

- Not letting any friends really know me

- What other choices do I make?

How Do You Make Better Choices?

You've figured out that you're not being nice to yourself right now—that's a first step. Now move on to helping yourself make healthier choices. Sometimes, knowing that someone else cares about you helps you to make healthy choices for yourself. There are people who care about you—maybe people you haven't even met yet, and somewhere inside yourself, you care, too. Otherwise you wouldn't be reading this book. If someone helped you find this book, then there's a person who cares. It's hard to let other people in and trust them when someone has taken advantage of you—really hard if it was someone who was supposed to care about you. That can be partly why you get really mad about being abused—because you found out that something you thought or felt was true wasn't. It's hard to feel safe and centered when you don't know what to believe anymore. Figuring out what makes you happy, learning healthy ways to cope, and expressing yourself helps you find out what to believe.

Easy Ways to Start Taking Care of Yourself

■ Stop doing the things in the unhealthy choices list (really, this one is hard, but just thinking about it is the first step).

■ Make a list of things you like about yourself (it's okay if there's only one thing on the list—that might be reading this book).

■ Start each day saying one good thing about yourself (maybe the only thing is that you take three deep breaths and decide to the face the day—that's okay! It's a start.).

■ Begin thinking about goals for yourself—what kind of person you want to be. Write it down, get a picture of it in your head.

■ Be nice to yourself every day—don't continue the abuse now that it has stopped.

Remind yourself:
"I'm choosing to make positive changes in my life."

Taking back control of your own life is one way to begin making healthy choices after being abused. This book has talked about lots of different ways to take back control of your life—taking back control of your feelings, taking back control of your behaviors and choices, taking back control of your relationships, taking back control of the direction of your life. Being able to start taking back control in any of these areas means taking care of yourself. That's healthy.

***

Being aware that you have choices can be a very powerful feeling. It can empower you in your healing journey. Change can be exciting, especially when it happens as a result of your own actions. I hope you're feeling good about all the positive changes you're making. This can be the beginning of an exciting time in your life, or at least a time of healthy change.

Let It Out

Remember, writing in a journal is a great way to help you figure exactly what's going on in your life and how you feel about it. It's private and usually feels like a safer place to start than talking to someone face-to-face. It's okay if you don't feel ready to do any journaling. Respect yourself and your own pace. Just do those things that you feel ready to do.

- List unhealthy choices that you plan to change.

- What are some healthy choices that you can make instead?

- What specific steps will you take to make these new choices?

- What things are you leaving behind as you start this new phase in your life—people, places, feelings, old parts of yourself?

CHAPTER 18

Rediscovering You and Moving On

To heal—to get to a place where the abuse doesn't affect you so deeply—means finding healthy ways to look at your experiences. It means learning:

- to accept what's happened to you, no matter how hard that is

- to work through and let go of some of the feelings about yourself and the abuse, and toward the abuser

- healthy ways of making choices for yourself—to set goals that will help you live your life the way you want to

- to feel good about yourself

Part of what you're doing is rediscovering who you are, which may feel out of sync with what your friends are doing. It may seem like they already know who they are, and it may even appear that you do, but how much of what you show to others is a mask?

It's okay to be figuring out who you are and what you like now. There are huge reasons you couldn't do it earlier. Being different is part of what makes everybody unique and special—more interesting and fun.

Figuring out new things I like is so cool! I've tried dancing and photography—next year I'm even trying out for soccer.

—STACY, 15

Getting to Know Yourself

Talking about getting to know yourself might seem strange. But you may not know what kind of person you want to be or what makes you special. No problem—look outside yourself for a few moments and notice what kind of qualities people can have. Start small or start large, close to home or as far away as the international media. Now start making a list—in your mind or on paper—of people you admire. Start with those in your everyday life or the rich and famous. List as many people as you can think of. They can be as different or as alike as your taste dictates.

Once you have your list, start figuring out what it is that you admire about these people.

- Do you like their cool sense of fashion or music?
- Do they seem like they would be fun to hang out with?
- Do they have a great job?
- Are they smart?
- Do they help others?
- Do you admire their earning potential?
- Do they travel a lot?
- Do they remind you of someone you love and who loves you?
- Do you like the way you feel when you're around them?
- Are they funny?
- Are they a good cook?
- Can they build things?

It's kind of fun to see how varied your list can be—kind of like a Renaissance person, somebody who can do all kinds of things. Do you want to be a Renaissance person or a specialist who's really good at a few things? Use your list of things you admire about others as a place to start trying new things yourself. You can still enjoy lots of different activities even if your skills are just developing.

What do you already know about your strengths, talents, skills, and dreams? Write that down. Now compare the list of things you liked about your heroes with your list for yourself. Do you see any similarities between the two lists? Start a new list with those similarities at the top. Then write down the other items from both lists, in the order of what's most important to you. Put the things you admire most right under the similarities. This list contains the qualities of the person you want to become. It may take some time and research to develop all these skills and qualities, but you can do it. Here are some ways to begin your research:

- Ask your school counselor.

- Go to the library.

- Search online.

- Ask your parents or other adults in your life who you respect.

- Check out classes or community groups to investigate some of the things on your list.

As you try out these activities and qualities—ways of being—you can practice trusting your inner voice. Be true to what feels right as you explore all your options. If something doesn't feel quite right, keep trying until you find things that truly feel good and define who you are.

Remind yourself:
"I have exciting, interesting goals and dreams for my life."

Another part of figuring out who you are involves getting in touch with your feelings—something that's often hard for people who have been abused. The following exercise can help increase your awareness, comfort, and knowledge of your own feelings.

An Exercise for Getting to Know Your Feelings

Sometimes the experience of being abused makes it difficult to be aware of your own feelings. This exercise suggests some ways to increase your awareness of your own feelings. Take a few minutes when you're really curious about your feelings, and try this exercise in front of a mirror. Focus on matching your facial expressions with your feelings. Don't worry about how you look. Stand in front of a mirror. Make a happy face, and

continued ➡

pay attention to how it feels inside. How does your face look? How does your body look? What's your posture like? Does your "body language" or internal feelings fit with the emotion you're trying to express? As you repeat the exercise for other feelings (mad, sad, scared, bored, nervous), notice how closely your feelings match what you're trying to express. Also be aware if any of the feelings evoke a memory from the time you were being abused. Does anything look or feel familiar from that experience? You may notice a sick feeling that's opposite of the face you're trying to show. For example, if your abuser told you to "quit crying and put a smile on your face," you probably don't always feel happy when you're smiling—it may feel more mixed up internally. Notice these cues from your body and write about them in your journal.

What Is Self-Care?

Self-care—taking care of yourself—is an important part of living, but one that you probably haven't been taught much about, especially if you've been around abusive people. They're more interested in you taking care of their needs. So, taking care of yourself may be another one of those things that you need to learn. But it doesn't have to feel overwhelming. Self-care can be fun and rejuvenating, once you let yourself believe that you're worth it—and you are.

Taking care of yourself can have many benefits. How you treat yourself often influences how other people treat you. Funny how that works, but if you take care of yourself and treat yourself with respect, then other people will likely treat you that way, too. One of the things you may find hard about taking care of yourself is believing that it's okay to do things for yourself and that you're worth it. These two obstacles to self-care are directly related to being abused. The experience of being abused can make you feel worthless. Those feelings get in the way of being able to do things for yourself or taking care of yourself. They're examples of things you need to "unlearn."

Remind yourself:
"I'm a unique individual who deserves to be treated well."

Think about the people in your life who have made you feel important or good about yourself. Are they still in your life? If so, spend time with them. Being around people who treat you well helps you treat yourself well, too. Another "trick" to learning how to treat yourself better is to treat yourself like you would a friend. You're probably going to be supportive of a friend, right? You're going to forgive that person for little things you don't like or mistakes that happen. So treat yourself like you would a friend— becoming your own best friend is part of self-care.

Self-care also means taking care of your whole self—body, mind, and spirit. That includes:

- eating well

- doing some kind of exercise you enjoy

- reading or keeping yourself intellectually stimulated

- getting enough sleep

- spending time with loved ones and friends who make you feel good about yourself

- letting yourself dream big dreams for your future, and figuring out what needs to happen now to help you move closer to those dreams

Some people think of self-care as a positive form of self-discipline. At first, you do things for yourself because you know they're good. Eventually, you do them because they make you feel good about yourself. Self-care includes an excitement for living— seeing each day as an adventure. Is that something you can let yourself do?

As an exercise, take a piece of paper and begin writing down things you can do for yourself in each of these areas: body, mind, spirit, dreams, and goals. If you don't want to write these things down, then cut out pictures from magazines that represent taking care of yourself in each of the areas—sometimes it's easier to visualize yourself doing something if you have a picture. It might even help you come up with new self-care ideas.

Another part of taking care of yourself is allowing yourself to have fun—something that's hard to do when you're busy worrying about being abused. At this point, you may not even know what you like to do for fun. You may have adopted some of the unhealthy choices talked about in Chapter 17 to escape, but you're probably only doing those things because they're familiar to you— that's what you know how to do. Part of the fun of being your own person is the excitement (which sometimes feels a bit like being scared or nervous) of trying new things. Use that nervous energy to fuel your self-exploration. Have fun with it!

Here are some healthy ways to have fun:

- Play sports like basketball, baseball, tennis, golf, swimming, or volleyball

- Go for a walk with a friend, family member, or pet

- Paint a picture or draw a self-portrait

- Write a poem

- Read a magazine

- Bake a cake

- Volunteer at a kids' camp or at the humane society

- Make music or listen to a favorite song

- Watch a movie

- Join a community theatre

- Grow a flower

- Make a pillow

- Get out the inline skates, a skateboard, or a bike

- Go hiking

- Call your grandparents, or other adults who are really there for you

- Talk to a friend

- Enjoy life—the simple things

How Do You Let Go of Memories?

Sometimes when you're sleeping, your dreams may be interrupted by monsters or scary people. When you're awake, you may have strange thoughts or feelings, or memories of abuse. Any of these scary thoughts, images, or memories, especially if they happen often, can feel like major obstacles to accomplishing what you want in your life. Letting go of memories is part of the healing process, but that's hard to do when the memories are intrusive. How much do your memories intrude upon your life? Chapter 16 talked about flashbacks and post-traumatic stress. These are other names for memories that intrude upon your life. There are ways to deal with such memories, usually with the help of a therapist or counselor. As your healing progresses, the memories should become less frequent and intense. Until that happens, here are some ways to respond to intrusive memories:

- Distract yourself with something else that's going on in your life.

- Talk with someone.

- Do something you enjoy.

- Imagine how you'd like the dream to end, rather than the negative or difficult way that the nightmare or memory usually occurs.

- Journal about the memories as a way to release them. Releasing memories means getting to the point where they don't bother you every day like they might during your healing process. The memories will always be part of your personal history, but they will become more like other information you have about yourself from your past and will no longer be so disturbing.

My dad stopped abusing me a couple of years ago. The memories don't bother me as much as they used to—it's like they're almost gone now—not so much a part of me. It's like I'm getting them out of my

continued ➡

head, but it hasn't been easy to make them go away. I talked to my counselor. I used my journal. I felt a lot of pain, but now I am starting to feel better.
—CURTIS, 15

Recurring, intrusive memories may be related to unresolved feelings about what happened. Maybe you still blame yourself or question what you could have done to prevent the abuse. Those kinds of feelings are normal, but they also can be a connection that keeps the memories fresh in your mind. The abuse wasn't your fault! You can't go back and change what happened, but you can change how you feel about yourself. One of the first things is to keep reminding yourself that the abuse was not your fault. That will help you let go of the memories. Nobody asks to be hit. Nobody asks to have sex when they're five, or forced into it at any age. Nobody asks to be called dumb or worthless. You're valuable just as you are.

Remind yourself:
"I can let go of the past."

It can be hard to forgive someone who abused you, and it's completely your decision about whether you do so. Some people feel pressured to forgive others because of religious or family beliefs. You don't have to forgive the abuser. But letting go of your feelings is important to your healing. Learning how to let go of feelings can be a healthy way to cope. Some people call that kind of letting go "forgiving," and it feels okay. Other people feel that forgiving is giving up. As you continue to let go of feelings, forgiving the abuser may eventually began to feel like a "normal" thing to do. That usually means that you're ready to forgive—that's the best time for you do to that—if that's what feels right for you.

Some people think it's important to confront the abuser, as part of their healing process. If you're thinking about a face-to-face confrontation, it's important to consider your reasons for wanting to do so. Think carefully about what you want to gain from such a conversation. If you choose to talk to your abuser, that person may not say the things you want to hear—he or she may blame you for telling or may not be able to take responsibility for the abuse. If you feel the abuser cannot hear what you have to say and be supportive, then you probably shouldn't confront this person directly. If you are worried about how the abuser will react if you choose to confront him or her, it may be a better idea not to confront. Remember that you may not get the reaction that you want. Consult a trusted adult or counselor to help you work through your feelings about confronting the abuser. You can confront the abuser in a therapeutic letter (see page 175), and that may be the safest and healthiest choice for you.

Being able to let go of old feelings and behaviors puts you in control—not the person who abused you. Being able to let go of memories makes room for all the new dreams you're working toward.

How Do You Build Healthy Relationships?

Part of your new dreams may include building healthy relationships. That's great, but it might feel a little scary because you're not sure what a healthy relationship is or how to be in one. Trusting yourself and your feelings is important in healthy relationships. You've been practicing that already, so you've got a good start. You may not trust yourself every time just yet, and that's okay. It takes time to learn new ways of doing things and new ways of being.

Respect and privacy are essential in healthy relationships. It may be difficult for you to imagine having respect or privacy, and being in relationships that include these things will probably be uncomfortable at first. For example, privacy may feel like the other person doesn't want to be around you. It could feel like too much emotional distance at first because you may be used to relationships with no boundaries—it may take a little time to get used to. Respect often involves listening to what others are asking. For example, if someone asks to be left alone or says he or she can't get together because of homework, you're respecting that person if you say it's okay. You may feel disappointed, and it's okay to tell your friend how you feel, but it's respectful to be supportive of what others need for themselves. By learning how to do this for your friends, you'll be learning how to do this for yourself as well.

As you're learning more about yourself, you can use that knowledge to communicate to others what you need to feel safe and good about yourself. Asking for respect and for the time you need for yourself are important ways to take care of yourself and to have healthy relationships. People who care about you will want to help you feel good and will try to respect your boundaries if you ask them. That's how healthy relationships work.

Dating

Sometimes people who have been abused let dating partners take advantage of them. It might feel so good to be close to someone that you forget to take care of yourself, because setting boundaries can make you feel alone again. Instead, you slip back into old patterns and let others abuse you again. You might be confusing comfort and familiarity with what feels right—and sometimes it's hard to know the difference. For example, you might feel as if you're doing what you want or being true to yourself by having sex or doing drugs because it feels good in the moment. Learning how to tell the difference is part of trusting yourself and setting appropriate boundaries—figuring out what's right for you includes knowing where you stop and someone else starts.

Establishing Boundaries

Establishing boundaries that feel safe is an important challenge for people who have experienced abuse. You can think of boundaries as a "personal space bubble" around you. This can be a physical space—about three feet around your body—but it may also include emotional or psychological space.

If you've been abused, you may feel very sensitive to what others want, instead of listening to what feels right for you. Again, you may have lost—or never developed—the ability to tell where your needs stop and other people's needs start. People who abuse usually try to make you think that your own feelings are not right or that something bad will happen if you listen to your own feelings. They don't want you to listen to yourself because then you're not listening to them. Once you start listening to yourself, you begin to take care of yourself. This will feel strange at first, but it gets easier with practice.

> About 1:15 in the morning, the phone rang. It was one of my close friends—well, actually he used to be my boyfriend, and I knew he was just calling to have sex. He was asking if he could come over. I told him no. I decided I wasn't going to be used like that anymore, and that felt good.
>
> —FELICIA, 16

Learning to trust your feelings is exactly what setting boundaries is about. Nobody can do that for you. You may feel confused about those feelings at first, but with time, you'll know when it's right to trust them. You'll be able to tell which feelings are out of habit (what you learned from being abused and are just used to doing) and which feelings are about you and what you really want for yourself.

Ways to Set Boundaries and Trust Yourself

- Say "no" when that's what you're feeling.
- Practice doing what feels right to you.
- Ask for help when you're confused.
- Practice being aware of your body (for example, noticing how your body experiences stress, such as holding it in your shoulders, or feeling a nervous stomach).

- Learn what those physical signals mean (start with feelings that are easier for you to notice, such as sadness or happiness).
- Expand your self-awareness to notice times when you're being incongruent or inconsistent within yourself—for example, when you're smiling but don't feel happy, or when someone asks how you are and you say "fine," but that's not how you really feel.

You're learning lots of new things, and that may feel overwhelming or draining. Maybe you don't feel you're making the kind of progress you would like to—like things are going too slowly. It's important to remember that everyone heals differently. Maybe the exercises that you've tried so far just don't feel right for you. Try the next one for building trust and self-knowledge. Those are important parts of feeling good about yourself and being in healthy relationships. You'll learn new skills, ways of being, and be able to make changes in your life as you're ready to do so. Be patient with yourself, as you would be with a friend. Remember, you're learning how to trust yourself, too. Therapy can be a good place to experience what a healthy relationship feels like. You can learn about boundaries and practice letting another person know how you feel, which are good starting places for a healthy relationship.

Developing Self-Knowledge and Trust

So you might be wondering how to start trusting yourself. That's a very good question, and one that has a different answer for everyone. One way to begin trusting yourself is to pay more attention to your feelings and reactions to yourself and others. For example, be aware of how you feel when somebody asks you to do something. Do you notice that you're feeling kind of blank or numb, or are you aware of feeling a little nervous—especially if you're telling somebody "no," or taking care of yourself in some other way? Doing something differently often creates a feeling of anxiety or nervousness that may feel similar to doing something wrong. That nervous feeling can become a new marker for you as you try to do things differently. If you're feeling a little nervous, maybe you can continue doing what you're doing instead of stopping—at least for a little while. If that nervous feeling is from doing something differently, the feeling will go away as you feel more comfortable with your new choices. Old feelings from abuse can often interfere with learning to trust yourself. It can take a period of "re-learning" before you're sure the feelings are your own and not left over from the abuse.

"Numb" feelings are an old protective mechanism from the abuse as well. Pushing through the numbness to know what you're really feeling may require cooperative work with a therapist or counselor before you can begin recognizing your own feelings. The numb feelings are part of how you protected yourself during the abuse, and sometimes it's difficult to give up something that has protected you in the past.

continued ➡

Try being aware of your reactions to people, places, and new situations. The more you are able to increase your awareness of feelings, thoughts, and reactions of your body, the more you are improving your ability to trust yourself. Examples of clues to be aware of within yourself include a nervous feeling in your stomach, tightness in your chest, a headache, a surge of anger, a wave of sadness or fear, or tiny negative messages that pop into your head. Becoming aware of all these clues will help you become more sure of yourself. You will become more aware of what makes you feel bad and what can help you feel good. Feeling more sure of who you are and learning what you can do to make yourself feel better will help you feel grounded within yourself. That kind of self-knowledge becomes a strength, and helps you live your life in a positive, authentic way, following what's important for you. Trusting yourself helps you begin to trust others, too, as you chart your direction for yourself.

Should You Set Goals for Your Future?

Setting goals is the first step in the process of making your dreams come true. First, you have to imagine what you want to accomplish or become, and then you have to come up with a plan to reach the goal or make that dream a reality. The goals may be really small like changing your daily routine, or they may be really big and sort of unclear for now. Either way is okay—we're just talking about finding yourself—finding out what makes you happy. Having goals of learning more about yourself and life may fit best for you right now. Continue exploring the lists you have made about goals and skills you want to develop. They'll help you remember your direction, even on those days when things get hard again. And remember, goals can always be changed. Tomorrow you may learn about something you didn't even know existed and it might change everything. Be open to possibilities.

You'll have some down days—everyone does—just don't get stuck there. Sometimes the list of goals, dreams, or even affirmations included in this book will carry you through on those rough days. Your healing will continue—things will feel better again. That's part of the healing process, and life itself really—we all have good and bad days. It's a journey that can have detours or that can feel like being lost. It may take a while to find the right path again.

That's okay. Look to your list of fun activities or coping skills on those down days. All the hard work you've done in this book can be kind of like a life preserver on those days when you feel like you're sinking back down. You're not alone—people care about you, and maybe the most helpful thing for you on those days will be something you've created yourself—all the work in the pages of this book. That's an amazing piece of your self-care program right there—already done for you by you.

Remind yourself:
"I'm learning healthy ways to take care of myself."

***

You've accomplished so much by reading this book. Whatever actions, exercises, journaling, or talking you have done as a result are an important part of your healing process. I hope you're beginning to feel the benefits of some of your hard work. Feeling good about the work you've already done can help you stay motivated as you continue the hard work of healing. Remember that you are not alone in the process—there are lots of people who want to support you and help you. You deserve to feel good about yourself and to have others treat with you respect. Hopefully, you're beginning to feel some of these positive changes in relationships with those around you as well.

> I met with my therapist for a couple of years before I really started noticing that I was feeling better. Sure, I still have some down days, but having people around who care about me helps keep me going.
>
> —Erin, 17

Life is a journey. Healing is a journey. Look how far you've come and what you've accomplished. You're a special traveler in that journey called your life, and you're taking control through your hard work and dreams. I wish you all the best as you continue your journey, follow your heart, and fulfill your dreams.

Let It Out

Remember, writing in a journal is a great way to help you figure exactly what's going on in your life and how you feel about it. It's private and usually feels like a safer place to start than talking to someone face-to-face. It's okay if you don't feel ready to do any journaling. Respect yourself and your own pace. Just do those things that you feel ready to do.

- List ways it may be hard for you to set boundaries in close relationships, like dating. Write down things you could say to reinforce your boundaries with others, showing your respect for yourself. For example, you might say, "No, I'm not ready to be that close yet. Let's go a little slower."

- Create an ideal me/self collage. On a piece of posterboard, paste or tape pictures from magazines of things you might want to do or learn more about. Include heroes/people you want to be like, things you want to do, and new things/activities to explore.

Resources

Hotlines

Alcohol Hotline
1-800-ALCOHOL (1-800-252-6465)
This national hotline features a trained staff that is ready 24 hours a day to help individuals with alcohol or drug problems. Whether looking for a treatment center or simply an honest talk with a counselor, this hotline can provide assistance.

Depression and Bipolar Support Alliance Information Line
1-800-826-3632
www.dbsalliance.org
Not a hotline, this information line fields requests for free information about mood disorders. You can also visit their Web site to find out about programs and support groups as well as information about depression, bipolar disorder, and the full spectrum of mood disorders.

Gay and Lesbian National Hotline
1-888-THE-GLNH (1-888-843-4564)
www.glnh.org
This national toll-free number is available Monday through Friday from 4 P.M. to midnight and Saturday from noon to 5 P.M. EST. Peer counselors provide advice, answers to your questions, and the opportunity to discuss problems safely and confidentially. You can also visit the Web site for further resources.

Girls and Boys Town National Hotline—Crisis Intervention Hotline
1-800-448-3000
www.girlsandboystown.org
Available 24 hours a day, this hotline offers crisis intervention and referrals for confronting abuse, addiction, depression, and other difficulties. You can also visit online to chat with professional counselors, learn about nationwide recovery programs, and find further resources for moving past abuse.

National Drug and Alcohol Treatment Referral
1-800-662-HELP (1-800-662-4357)
www.drugabuse.gov
Operated by the U.S. Department of Health and Human Services, this toll-free automated service offers substance abuse information and alcohol treatment referrals. Visit the Web site for information about the different kinds of drugs, their effects on the body, and ways to combat addiction.

National Referral Network for Kids in Crisis
1-800-KID-SAVE (1-800-543-7283)
Sometimes it really is necessary to seek professional help when dealing with problems you face. This referral line provides contact information for mental health, drug abuse, and other medical facilities in your area.

Books

Everything You Need to Know About Drug Abuse by Arthur G. Herscovitch (New York: Rosen Publishing Group, 1999). Find straightforward information on all of the different types of drugs: how they affect your body and mind, the potential consequences teens may not be ready for, and advice and alternatives for avoiding them altogether.

Highs! Over 150 Ways to Feel Really, REALLY Good . . . Without Alcohol or Other Drugs by Alex J. Packer (Minneapolis: Free Spirit Publishing, 2000). Use safe and creative ways to find peace, pleasure, excitement, and insight. Find highs involving sports, exercise, food, the senses, nature, family, friends, and more; the best part is that all of these methods are completely drug-free.

Taking Charge of My Mind & Body: A Girls' Guide to Outsmarting Alcohol, Drug, Smoking, and Eating Problems by Gladys Folkers and Jeanne Engelmann (Minneapolis: Free Spirit Publishing, 1997). First-person stories and current research empower you to take charge of your life, avoiding the pitfalls of alcohol, nicotine, and other drugs.

Taste Berries for Teens: Inspirational Short Stories and Encouragement on Life, Love, Friendship, and Tough Issues compiled by Bettie B. Youngs and Jennifer Leigh Youngs with contributions from teens for teens (Deerfield Beach, FL: Health Communications, 1999). Read about others' best and worst times in this inspiring book for teens. A heartwarming read, discover how other teens deal with and overcome problems.

Write Where You Are: How to Use Writing to Make Sense of Your Life by Caryn Mirriam-Goldberg (Minneapolis: Free Spirit Publishing, 1999). Explore life's highs and lows through the medium of writing. Learn how to get started, explore your feelings, solve problems, and communicate clearly.

Web Sites

Gentle Touch's Web
www.gentletouchsweb.com
Find dozens of stories here from victims of abuse. If you feel comfortable doing so, you can even share your own.

National Institute on Drug Abuse
www.drugabuse.gov
This site provides statistics and information about drug abuse. Discover amazing facts that will make your answer to the drug question an easy "no." Related links offer more information about drugs and include resources for fighting addiction.

Online Depression Screening Test
www.med.nyu.edu/Psych/screens/depres.html
Located at the New York University Department of Psychiatry's Web site, this test is a very basic screening for symptoms of depression. It is not a formal psychiatric evaluation and cannot be a sole basis on which to determine whether you are depressed; only a qualified professional can accurately diagnose depression.

Outproud
www.outproud.org
This site features resources for gay, lesbian, bisexual, and transgender youth. Find reading lists, stories from other GLBT youth, discussion forums, and links to related sites.

Teens Health
www.kidshealth.org/teen
This site offers health information about every imaginable aspect of mental and physical health. Read about nutrition, drugs and alcohol, sexually transmitted diseases, safety, and more.

Organizations

Al-Anon/Alateen
1600 Corporate Landing Parkway
Virginia Beach, VA 23454
1-888-4AL-ANON (1-800-425-2666)
www.al-anon.alateen.org
Al-Anon works to help families and friends of alcoholics recover from the effects of living with the drinking problem of a relative or friend. Alateen is a recovery program for young people, offering them the opportunity to share and recover from their experiences with a friend or family member's drinking. Their toll-free number is available Monday through Friday from 8 A.M. to 6 P.M. EST.

American Psychiatric Association
1000 Wilson Boulevard, Suite 1825
Arlington, VA 22209
1-888-357-7924
www.psych.org
Contact this organization for the names and phone numbers of local psychiatrists. The information is also available at their Web site, along with information about mental health and support resources. Please note that the number listed is not a crisis line. If you are in danger or need to talk with someone, call 1-800-999-9999.

American Psychological Association
750 First Street NE
Washington, DC 20002
1-800-374-2721
www.apa.org
This organization provides information about psychological services, including fact sheets, a listing of professional services in your area, and guidelines for seeking treatment. Call, write, or visit their Web site for more information. Note that the number listed above is not a crisis line; if you need to talk with someone or are in danger, call 1-800-999-9999.

National Eating Disorders Association
603 Stewart Street, Suite 803
Seattle, WA 98101
(206) 382-3587
www.nationaleatingdisorders.org
Dedicated to eliminating eating disorders and body disatisfaction, the National Eating Disorders Association creates programs and curricula that increase the awareness of eating disorders. Call, write, or visit their Web site for current information about eating disorders and useful resources for combating body dissatisfaction.

Parents, Families and Friends of Lesbians and Gays (PFLAG)
1726 M Street NW, Suite 400
Washington, DC 20036
(202) 467-8180
www.pflag.org
A national organization, PFLAG celebrates diversity and advocates for respect, dignity, and equality for all human beings, regardless of sexual orientation or gender identity. Through mutual acceptance and understanding, PFLAG promotes healthy and positive home, school, and work environments. Call, write, or visit their Web site to locate a chapter near you.

Endnotes

Chapter 1

[1]National Child Abuse and Neglect Data System (NCANDS). Summary of Key Findings from Calendar Year 2000. Children's Bureau. Administration on Children, Youth, and Families. U.S. Dept. of Health and Human Services.

[2]Nancy Peddle and Ching-Tung Wang, *Current Trends in Child Abuse Reporting and Fatalities: The 1999 Fifty State Survey* (Chicago: Prevent Child Abuse America, 2001).

[3]Howard N. Snyder, *Sexual Assault of Young Children as Reported to Law Enforcement: Victim, Incident, and Offender Characteristics* (Pittsburg, PA: National Center for Juvenile Justice, 2000). *www.ojp.usdoj.gov/bjs/pub/pdf/saycrle.pdf*

[4]National Child Abuse and Neglect Data System (NCANDS). Summary of Key Findings from Calendar Year 1998. Children's Bureau. Administration on Children, Youth, and Families. U. S. Dept. of Health and Human Services. Reported in *Juvenile Offenders and Victims: 1999 National Report. ncjrs.org/html/ojjdp/nationalreport99/toc.html.*

[5]L. K. Brown, K. J. Lourie, C. Zlotnick, J. Cohn, "Impact of Sexual Abuse on the HIV-Risk-Related Behavior of Adolescents," *American Journal of Psychiatry* 157, no. 9 (2000): 1413–15; K. S. Kendler, C. M. Bulik, J. Silberg, J. M. Hettema, J. Myers, C. A. Prescott, "Childhood Sexual Abuse and Adult Psychiatric and Substance Use Disorders in Women," *Archives of General Psychiatry* 57, no. 10 (2000): 953–59; D. Neumark-Sztainer, M. Story, P. J. Hannan, T. Beuhring, M. D. Resnick, "Disordered Eating Among Adolescents: Associations with Sexual/Physical Abuse and Other Familial/Psychosocial Factors," *International Journal of Eating Disorders* 28, no. 3 (2002): 249–58; S. A. Wonderlich, R. D. Crosby, J. E. Mitchell, J. A. Roberts, B. Haseltine, G. DeMuth, K. M. Thompson, "Relationship of Childhood Sexual Abuse and Eating Disturbance in Children," *Child and Adolescent Psychiatry* 39, no. 10 (2000): 1277–83.

[6]National Child Abuse and Neglect Data System (NCANDS). Summary of Key Findings from Calendar Year 2000. Children's Bureau. Administration on Children, Youth, and Families. U.S. Dept. of Health and Human Services.

Chapter 2

[1]National Child Abuse and Neglect Data System (NCANDS). Summary of Key Findings from Calendar Year 2000. Children's Bureau. Administration on Children, Youth, and Families. U.S. Dept. of Health and Human Services.

[2]B. A. Robinson. Ontario Consultants on Religious Tolerance. 2001. *www.religioustolerance.org/spankin2.htm*

[3]Robinson. Ontario Consultants on Religious Tolerance.

Chapter 3

[1]National Child Abuse and Neglect Data System (NCANDS). Summary of Key Findings from Calendar Year 2000. Children's Bureau. Administration on Children, Youth, and Families. U.S. Dept. of Health and Human Services.

[2]Howard N. Snyder, *Sexual Assault of Young Children as Reported to Law Enforcement: Victim, Incident, and Offender Characteristics* (Pittsburg, PA: National Center for Juvenile Justice, 2000). *www.ojp.usdoj.gov/bjs/pub/pdf/saycrle.pdf*

[3]Snyder, *Sexual Assault of Young Children as Reported to Law Enforcement.*

[4]Snyder, *Sexual Assault of Young Children as Reported to Law Enforcement.*

[5]Snyder, *Sexual Assault of Young Children as Reported to Law Enforcement.*

Chapter 5

[1]National Child Abuse and Neglect Data System (NCANDS). Summary of Key Findings from Calendar Year 2000. Children's Bureau. Administration on Children, Youth, and Families. U.S. Dept. of Health and Human Services.

Chapter 6

[1]Josephson Institute of Ethics, "Report Card on the Ethics of American Youth 2000 in School Safety Statistics," June 2001, National School Safety Center, Westlake Village, California. *www.nssc1.org*

Chapter 12

[1]U.S. Dept. of Health and Human Resources, Administration on Children, Youth and Families. *Child Maltreatment, 1999.* Washington, D.C. U.S. Government Printing Office, 2001.

Index

A

Abuse
and being drunk or high, 63–64
breaking a long-term pattern of,
67, 68
deaths from, 10
definition of, 9–10
effects of, 13
examples of, 12
experiencing more than one form
of, 12
getting help from state agencies,
17
incidence of, by ethnic origin, 19
incidence of, in boys *vs.* girls, 10
journaling about being a survivor
of, 20
learning to trust your inner voice,
75–76
reactions to
acting out the abuse, 15–16
feeling confused, 14
feeling numb or forgetting the
abuse, 13–14
feeling out of control, 16
feeling scared or worthless, 15
reasons for learning how to
think/talk about, 2
recognizing, 9
reports of, 10
state laws against, 17
vs. assault, 11
vs. experiencing conflict, 16, 18
vs. mistreatment or abusive
behavior by peers, 51
vs. normal parental actions and
expectations, 16–17
vs. violent/hurtful behavior by
similar-age peers, 10
See also Bullying; Date rape;
Emotional abuse; Neglect;
Physical abuse; Relationship
abuse; Sexual abuse

Abusers
brothers or sisters as, 63
characteristics of
emotional abusers, 40
physical abusers, 23
sexual abusers, 30
those who neglect, 47
chatroom acquaintances as,
66–67, 68
confronting, 193–194
examples of, 10
as liars, 72–75
parents as, 62
religious leaders as, 64–65
teachers/coaches as, 65
victims of abuse as, 66
who are drunk or high, 63–64
Acquaintance rape. *See* Date rape
Affirmations, 5–6
Al-Anon/Alateen, 203
Alcohol abuse, 179–180
Alcohol Hotline, 201
Allegations, definition of, 112
American Association of Suicidology,
89
American Psychiatric Association,
203
American Psychological Association,
204
Anorexia, 178
Assault, *vs.* abuse, 11

B

Back on Track (Wright), 133
Beating, 23–24
Blame, avoiding taking the
journaling about, 76
overcoming feelings of
responsibility, 69–70
recognizing lies about the abuse,
72–73
remembering that the abuser is
always at fault, 66, 69, 71

207

About the Author

Deanna Pledge, Ph.D., is a psychologist in private practice, an author, and an assistant professor at a local college and university in Columbia, Missouri. Her work with clients who have been abused spans a decade, in both private and public agency settings. Abuse is something that shouldn't happen to anyone. But it does. Working with her clients motivated Deanna to write this book. She wanted to provide a resource for teens—and those who care about them—to help them work through such difficult life experiences.

Deanna also conducts workshops on journaling and encourages everyone to explore personal creativity for their own mental health and healing. She works regularly with the media and develops training texts, articles, and books. Her professional writing includes the topics of family stress, mental health issues, therapeutic techniques, journal writing, personal growth, life transitions, and women's issues.

Other Great Books from Free Spirit

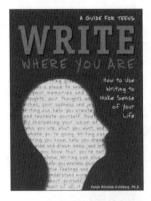

Write Where You Are
How to Use Writing to Make Sense of Your Life
by Caryn Mirriam-Goldberg, Ph.D.
This insightful book helps teens articulate and understand their hopes and fears, lives and possibilities through writing. Not just another writing skills book, it invites teens to make sense of their lives through writing—and shows them how. Recommended for young writers, English teachers, and writing instructors. For ages 12 & up.
$14.95; 168 pp.; softcover; illus.; 7¼" x 9"

Making the Most of Today
Daily Readings for Young People on Self-Awareness, Creativity, & Self-Esteem
by Pamela Espeland and Rosemary Wallner
Quotes from figures including Eeyore, Mariah Carey, and Dr. Martin Luther King Jr. guide you through a year of positive thinking, problem solving, and practical lifeskills—the keys to making the most of every day. For ages 11 & up.
$10.95; 392 pp.; softcover; 4¼" x 6¼"

To place an order or to request a free catalog of SELF-HELP FOR KIDS® and SELF-HELP FOR TEENS® materials, please write, call, email, or visit our Web site:

Free Spirit Publishing Inc.
217 Fifth Avenue North • Suite 200 • Minneapolis, MN 55401-1299
toll-free 800.735.7323 • local 612.338.2068 • fax 612.337.5050
help4kids@freespirit.com • www.freespirit.com

Visit us on the Web!
www.freespirit.com

Stop by anytime to find our Parents' Choice Approved catalog with fast, easy, secure 24-hour online ordering; "Ask Our Authors," where visitors ask questions—and authors give answers—on topics important to children, teens, parents, teachers, and others who care about kids; links to other Web sites we know and recommend; fun stuff for everyone, including quick tips and strategies from our books; and much more! Plus our site is completely searchable so you can find what you need in a hurry. Stop in and let us know what you think!

Just point and click!